A Dog
Year

A Dog Year

Rescuing Devon, the most troublesome dog in the world

JON KATZ

EBURY
PRESS

14

Published in 2008 by Ebury Press, an imprint of Ebury Publishing
A Random House Group Company
First published in the USA by Villard Books in 2002

Epigraph on page vii is reprinted from *Eminent Dogs, Dangerous Men* by Donald McCaig, by special arrangement with Lyons Press, New York, N.Y.

The Random House Group Limited Reg. No. 954009

Addresses for companies within the Random House Group can be found at
www.randomhouse.co.uk

A CIP catalogue record for this book is available from the British Library

The Random House Group Limited supports The Forest Stewardship Council (FSC), the leading international forest certification organisation. All our titles that are printed on Greenpeace approved FSC certified paper carry the FSC logo. Our paper procurement policy can be found at
www.rbooks.co.uk/environment

Printed in the UK by CPI Cox & Wyman, Reading, RG1 8EX

ISBN 9780091938680

To buy books by your favourite authors and register for offers visit
www.rbooks.co.uk

For Paula,
who loves dogs, but not this much

In our culture, humans with a special knack for animals have always been thought queer, or worse.

Learning a dog's worldview, altering it (within bounds), accepting a dog's understanding as sometimes more reliable than a man's—these commonplace tools of dog training are a mild cultural treason. . . . The truly dangerous inhabit a reality most of us can scarcely imagine—every day they share the thoughts, habits, tics and aspirations of a genuinely alien mind.

—Donald McCaig,
Eminent Dogs, Dangerous Men

CONTENTS

Introduction: Perfect Harmony xi

One: Welcome to Newark 1
Two: Oceangoing Labs 17
Three: Old Hemp and Old Kep 33
Four: Manic Panic 47
Five: On the Mountain 57
Six: Showdown in New Jersey 73
Seven: Lots and Lots and Lots of Heart 91
Eight: Weirdville 109
Nine: Homer 125
Ten: Coming and Going 137
Eleven: Poultrygeist 151
Twelve: Dog Days 159
Thirteen: Barbie Collies 175
Postscript 195

Caution 201
Afterword 203
Acknowledgements 215
About the Author 218

Introduction

PERFECT HARMONY

*W*hen I was in the fourth grade, I got up before dawn one morning, braving a bitter winter in Providence, Rhode Island, and headed for my elementary school to be sure that I was first in line.

The school janitor was giving away a puppy.

I waited, shivering, for several hours, fighting to defend my spot against some enormous sixth-graders. But I held my ground and brought home Lucky, also shivering, in a cardboard box. It was the happiest day of my life.

I can't remember what kind of dog he was, only that we'd had him for a few weeks when he got distemper, then disappeared. My parents told me that he was sick and had to recover on a farm out in the country, where he could roam freely.

Weeks later, in response to my badgering and increasingly

agitated demands to visit him, my father told me that Lucky was "very sick" and would have to stay on the farm for a long time, perhaps for good. Then he took me to Rigney's Ice Cream Parlor on Hope Street and bought me a black raspberry cone. Excursions with my father were a rare thing, reserved for the most extraordinary occasions. My father never said a word as we slurped our cones, and neither did I.

I was young but not stupid. It would be years before I loved any dog that much again.

♦♦♦♦♦♦♦♦♦

Next came Sam, the first dog who was more or less mine. He was an iron-willed basset hound with whom my mother warred relentlessly over where he slept (on my bed), where he napped (on the new living room sofa), and what he ate (anything that wasn't locked away).

Sam was fearless. Every time my mother pulled into the driveway, she looked up to see him relaxing on the new sofa, located in the bay window on the side of the house. By the time she rushed inside, he'd be sitting innocently on the floor, but she whaled him with a rolled-up newspaper anyway. I admired the way Sam stood up to her tirades and temper and took his medicine. He never flinched, ran, or hid; nor did he ever stop dozing on the couch.

One Friday night, with about fifteen members of our extended family gathered around my mother's new dining room table, which sat proudly atop a new Oriental carpet she had saved for years to buy, Sam calmly strolled up, put his front paws on the table, clamped his strong jaws onto the steaming pot roast, and yanked it away.

My grandmother, who didn't believe that Jews ought to have dogs in the first place, started screaming in Yiddish.

Clearly Sam's plan was to light out for the basement—the door was just a few feet away—where he'd wolf down as much meat as possible before the authorities caught up with him. He never got that far.

My mother, shrieking in fury, headed him off at the kitchen doorway and Sam led her on a desperate chase around the table, dragging the meat with him, leaving a trail of gravy and grease along her new carpet.

I don't know how long this would have gone on—we were all too astonished by Sam's daring act to move, and my sister and I were silently rooting for him anyway—but my big brother finally knocked his chair over to block Sam's route and tackled him.

Even as he went down and was hauled off in a din of curses, whacks, and recriminations, Sam was gobbling as much of the entrée as he could. He had calculated the price, weighed the odds, and gone for it. Sam was the bravest dog I ever knew.

His obstinacy could be irritating, of course. Every night, Sam climbed onto my bed, positioned himself between me and the wall, and began pushing me toward the edge. But if I tried to shove him back, he'd nip my hand and growl me away. Once or twice a week he'd muscle me right off onto the floor. If anybody came in to see what caused the thump, Sam would be snoring peacefully.

We moved to New Jersey when I was in high school. In the days of packing and farewells beforehand, Sam suddenly vanished. My mother was vague about where he had gone. At first, she said, she had tried to give him to a neighbor, but he'd immediately bitten every person in the family, which sounded like Sam, all right. So she'd found him a farm in northern Rhode Island where he could, she said, roam freely.

I wish I had gotten to say goodbye.

❖❖❖❖❖❖❖❖

There have been others. Before Lucky, my family had included a foul-tempered German shepherd named King, who regularly took off after milkmen and mail carriers until my mother sorrowfully had to send him away. After my wife and I married, we adopted a russet-colored mutt named Bean who looked like a fox. She kept us faithful company for years but was more my wife's dog than mine. Clarence was a crotchety golden retriever bought on impulse at a puppy mill; I loved him despite his grumpiness and many health problems.

Once in a great while, however, the right person is fortunate enough to get the right dog, to have the time to take care of it, to connect with it in a profound way. It takes a confluence of luck and timing, being at a particular point in life that coincides with the nature, breeding, and disposition of a particular dog. By the spring of 2000, I was lucky enough to have not one but two dogs with whom I had come to live in great harmony, two genial, pure-bred yellow Labrador retrievers I'd gotten from a breeder in northern New Jersey.

All the things that needed to converge did. I was working at home, writing. The dogs were attentive, smart, calm, and loving. They also had that meditative Lab quality of being able to disappear into themselves for extended periods, leaving me in peace when I needed it.

I hired a trainer to train me, to teach me to teach them how to come, sit, stay, lie down, and walk reliably beside me without leashes. Professional dog trainers and handlers understand that their real work is to train dogs' owners. Dogs more or less know what they need to do. The issue is almost always how to communicate what you want from them, in a positive yet effective way. It cost a few hundred dollars, and most people will tell you it isn't worth it, but they are dead wrong. When it comes to dogs, it was the best buy of my life, returning the cost with interest in myriad ways.

We hardly had a bad moment, the three of us, so neatly did we fit together, interlocking pieces of the puzzle that is the varied partnership between humans and dogs.

Julius and Stanley embodied the noblest characteristics of their proud breed. They were handsome, loyal, utterly dependable, and affectionate. Julius came first. My daughter was young, and while there are different viewpoints about this, I personally don't believe there's a more rewarding moment for a parent than handing a happy, squirming, doe-eyed Lab puppy over to a small kid. I carry the look on her face in my memory, and while there are times when I can't remember what day of the week it is, I can always recall the wonder and joy in her eyes as if it had just happened.

Although I bought the dog with my daughter in mind, she was soon playing computer games and collecting garish-looking dolls, and I was out in the chill winter mornings cheering and exulting when a puzzled but earnest puppy took a dump outside.

Julius became mine, of course, the two of us bonding as if by Krazy Glue.

A year later, the breeder called and invited me to take a ride with my daughter to see the new litter. I was just looking, I assured my muttering and incredulous wife, Paula, who'd dragged Julius's old plastic dog crate out of the basement, ready to house its new resident, before I'd left the driveway.

My daughter and I returned with tiny, heart-melting Stanley.

Julius was initially dubious about this new pest he had to contend with, but within a couple of days the two Labs loved each other as much as I loved them both, and they loved me and my family and, well, everybody who passed by.

It was a happy relationship from the first, and it only grew better, more comfortable. Both dogs were housebroken within days, settling happily into hours of rawhide-chewing.

Our lifestyles, as they say, meshed perfectly. Neither dog had much interest in running around.

Their great genius was doing nothing in particular with great style and dedication. Both disdained traditional canine tasks such as pursuing squirrels or rabbits, digging, or destroying property. Their chosen work was to reflect on the state of the world, lick neighborhood kids, and accompany me through midlife.

In the morning, neither dog moved a muscle until I did; then both slithered into bed for a family cuddle. After I was up and dressed, they sat quietly and attentively beneath the kitchen table, staring hypnotically at their food bowls, as if the power of their gazes would conjure up something tasty.

After breakfast, the early walk through our pleasant suburban neighborhood was leisurely, Julius and Stanley forensically sniffing along behind. Certain shrubs and rocks were always carefully inspected, each at a quite deliberate pace, the only area in which they would not compromise. Nothing could rush them; they'd go over every millimeter of a sapling's bark, undistractedly, until satisfied. A rabbit could hop right by—and sometimes did—without interrupting them.

For a half hour or so, the dogs proceeded at such stately paces and behaved so dependably that I was free to think about the coming day, what I wanted to write, how I wanted to write it. Our walks were tranquil, interrupted only by a stream of friends and admirers, from dog buddies to school-bus drivers.

Despite their historic roles as hunting dogs, however, they disdained rain and snow, and in inclement weather mastered a convenient hundred-yard dash to the nearest tree, then turned and hustled back inside.

Then it was time for work. I prepared a sandwich for each, taking two big rawhide chews and slathering a layer of peanut butter in between. Jules and Stanley carried the concoctions to the backyard and settled in for a deliberate gnaw, after which they were spent, and needed to refresh themselves with a long rest.

If the weather was fine, the dogs would spend much of the morning dozing in the yard. They might rouse themselves to bark at a passing dog. Mostly not.

On unpleasant days, they came into my study and offered themselves as footrests, both tucked underneath my desk, one on my left, one on my right.

I never had to provide much in the way of instruction. These guys knew how to relax. When the computer chimed as it booted up (I am an unswerving Macintosh man), the dogs dropped to the floor as if they'd been shot. They didn't move until they heard the monitor thunk off, at which point they'd rise (cautiously), ready for another stroll.

After a year or so, Julius and Stanley had achieved a Labrador state of grace, the ability to become an organic part of your life rather than an intrusion into it.

For a writer, having two such quiet and patient companions is a godsend. They warded off loneliness. They also kept me from a purely sedentary existence. After lunch, we'd rack up another mile or two at our usual unhurried pace.

Through the day, I supplied rawhide chews, pigs' ears, indeterminable and smelly dried bull parts, and a rain of treats and biscuits. It was ridiculously indulgent, of course, but I could not do enough for these boys, nor they for me. I tried to repay them for their love and unflagging loyalty, even though that was unnecessary and impossible.

They had their idiosyncracies. Julius was so unconcerned about wildlife (the sort his brethren traditionally retrieved) that he'd been known to nap inches from a rabbit's nest in the garden. And when Stanley wanted to chase a ball—which was much of the time—he would nip me in the butt to get me moving.

Once in a great while somebody would strew the garbage around the house, in the centuries-old tradition of Labs in Newfoundland who worked with fishermen, loved the cold, wet outdoors, and had to forage for food; they got to be pretty flexible about what they'd put in their stomachs. If I left them alone in the house, they collected odd articles of clothing—my wife's fuzzy bedroom slippers were a favorite—and slept with them.

It had been years since either dog had been on a leash or given me reason, despite the technicalities of local leash laws, to use one. Every kid in the neighborhood knew them and waved at them from bikes and car windows, through soccer-field fences. For many, they provided the first introduction to dogs, and they set a high standard. Over the years, many people told me that Julius or Stanley had inspired them to go out and get a dog.

When night fell, so did the Labs, settling on their cedar beds for a final rawhide snack, and descending into a deep, unmoving sleep.

After some years—Stanley was seven and Julius eight—we moved almost like a school of fish, the three of us veering in one direction, then another. We turned corners at the same time, sat in various parks and yards sharing lunch.

All the one ever asked was to live, play, and work alongside me. All the other one wanted besides that was the chance to swim in ponds once in a while and chase a ball a few times a day. They got what they wanted. So did I.

Of the various dogs in my life, Julius and Stanley were the first with whom I lived in such tranquillity. They transformed me from a dog owner into a dog lover. The three of us were as settled in our relationship as a middle-aged man and his dogs could be. Perhaps too settled.

John Steinbeck once wrote that it was the nature of humans as they grew older to complain about change, especially change for the better. I have never really had that particular problem. Change loves me, defines and stalks me like a laser-guided smart bomb. It comes at me in all forms, suddenly and with enormous impact, from making shifts in work to having and raising a kid to buying a cabin on a distant mountaintop. Sometimes, change comes on four legs.

One

WELCOME TO NEWARK AIRPORT

He was a two-year-old border collie of Australian lineage, well-bred but high-strung, and in big trouble. He had been shown at obedience trials in the Southwest. But something had gone very wrong with this arrangement and his breeder had taken him back and was working to find him a home. He needed one badly, she told me. That was all I knew about Devon when I drove to Newark Airport to pick him up.

I already had two sweet dogs and I had plenty of non-dog-related responsibilities as well. I wasn't particularly keen on taking in a third dog.

But this breeder, who kept a fierce eye on her dogs even after they'd left her kennels, had been e-mailing me for a while. She'd read a book of mine called *Running to the Mountain,* which mentioned my Labs Julius and Stanley.

She called me up; before long we were spending hours on the phone. Deanne wasn't pushing me, she kept saying, but she believed this dog belonged with me. She meant to make it happen.

I'd been fascinated by border collies for years, poring over books like *The Versatile Border Collie* by Janet Larson, browsing Web sites where owners post stories of their dogs' weird behavior, exchanging tentative e-mails with breeders. They were such intelligent dogs, I'd read, and somehow exotic. But everyone I consulted said more or less the same thing: unless you have a hundred acres right outside your back door, don't do it. I had only a normal suburban New Jersey yard—and did I mention that I already had two large dogs?

So I hemmed and hawed about adopting a border collie, especially one with more than the usual . . . issues. A part of me was drawn to the idea, but the rational part said: Stop! Danger ahead!

Deanne was patient, persuasive, persistent without being pushy, a subtle line she walked with great skill. The better we got to know each other, the more effective her message. Devon, she said, was a special case in need of special handling. He was uncommonly bright, willful, and emotionally beat up. From my book, with its descriptions of Julius and Stanley and of my cabin in rural upstate New York—close to border collie nirvana—she suspected that I had a high tolerance for odd dog behavior. And Devon was, well, odd.

After a few weeks of this back-and-forth, she put him on a plane and shipped him from Lubbock, Texas, eastward to his new life. On a balmy spring night, I stood outside the American Airlines baggage freight window in Terminal B.

Waiting nervously, I recalled in particular the warning of breeder and author Larson. She was straightforward: "In border collies, the wild type or wolf temperament is common and seems to be genetically linked to the herding behavior. This means that many border collies make unstable pets, and some can be dangerous. Remember that these dogs were developed as sheep herders, and in the mountains and moors they did not need to be sociable with strangers. As a result, shy and sharp temperaments are fairly common."

In my thickly settled neighborhood only about fifteen miles west of New York City, you don't encounter many mountains or moors. You don't see many border collies, either.

Doing my homework had only increased my trepidation. Border collies need vast spaces to roam, I read. They had insatiable energy; they'd go nuts living out the fate of many suburban family hounds: locked in crates or basements all day while the grown-ups worked; never properly trained, socialized, or exercised; growing increasingly neurotic while the kids, for whose sake the dogs were allegedly acquired, often wound up ignoring them.

Border collies, I read further, sometimes mistook kids for sheep and nipped or bit them. They had peculiar habits, interests, needs, and mood swings. Working dogs in every sense of the word, diggers and foragers, they abhorred loneliness and inactivity and hated having nothing to do. If you didn't give them something to keep them occupied, they would find something themselves.

They often had trouble with other dogs, herding or chasing them. They obsessively pursued squirrels, rabbits, chipmunks, cars, and trucks—that is to say, anything that moved quickly away from them. Always in pursuit of something mobile, they'd take off explosively when they found it, racing after it at blinding speeds. Once launched, few things—shrubbery, fences, traffic, shouts—could slow them down.

❖❖❖❖❖❖❖❖❖

Newark Airport is a sometimes overwhelming place, justly famous for its nearly continual mobs, traffic, congestion, and delays. Devon's plane had been routed through Atlanta, and the airport monitors said that his flight would be late, though not how late. This had to be rough on any dog, let alone a wired-up border collie with a delicate psychological history. Poor guy. I pictured him in the dark hold, feeling the plane move, the crates and luggage vibrating as the deafening engine roared nearby. Terminal B was unlikely to be a welcoming destination, either.

I had only the vaguest sense of what this dog looked like. I'd declined Deanne's offer of a photograph, mostly because I didn't want to make an adoption decision based on looks. That was a bad reason, I thought, to get a dog.

Parts of his story were vague. He had never lived in a house much or, I gathered, had a single human to attach himself to. He'd been neutered only a couple of weeks earlier, by the owner, before she gave him back to Deanne. The usually routine surgery had gone badly: the vets couldn't put him to sleep with the usual amount of anesthesia, so they increased the dosage, and then they almost couldn't wake him up. He was iron-willed and smart.

"Devon's got some things to deal with," Deanne told me. My understanding was that Devon had been raised for obedience competition, had fallen short in some way and been replaced. This wasn't an uncommon fate in obedience show dogs, who aren't raised to be pets. When they fail—and they know when they fail—they have no real purpose.

So Devon had languished. "He needs somebody to connect to," Deanne told me. "He's discouraged."

She also told me I could change his name—it *was* a tad Martha Stewart for my taste—but I figured he'd have enough to adjust to.

Border collie breeders are notoriously picky, since so many

of their weird and energetic animals wind up abandoned or unwanted. I suspect they tend to look either for ranchers with hordes of sheep or stay-at-home oddballs—writers, for example—to take in the rejects.

It seemed that when I'd mentioned—during the interminable interviewing any potential border collie owner is subjected to—that Stanley liked to give my butt a nibble when he wanted me to throw his ball, that clinched something for Deanne. You had to have an unusual sense of humor, she said, to appreciate border collies. So Devon was en route. I'm still not entirely sure why I agreed.

What would this do to Julius and Stanley, who had placid dog lives filled with chewbones, stuffed toy animals, strolls to the park, and regular retreats upstate, where Stanley loved to swim while Julius stared happily at the mountaintop at nothing in particular for hours? They enjoyed the finest hypoallergenic lite dog food; summer vacations on Cape Cod; four, sometimes five walks a day and round-the-clock companionship with each other. They'd returned these favors with nothing but love and loyalty.

I had left them in the yard that night, where they could meet Devon. Given a bit of space, perhaps nobody would get territorial or testy.

"Boys," I'd announced solemnly, "I'm bringing another dog here, Devon. He might be a little wacky. Be patient." Julius and

Stanley looked at me fondly, both tails wagging. They were nothing if not patient.

I had put a bowl and a jug of water in my minivan, along with a small bag of biscuits. I was holding a new blue leash and collar, to which I'd already attached a dog tag with Devon's name and my phone numbers.

I felt anxious, dubious, excited, strongly pulled toward something that made no sense. It was not much comfort to hear that Deanne had promised I could send the dog back to her if he couldn't adapt.

❖❖❖❖❖❖❖❖❖

An hour after I arrived, the plane landed. Pacing nervously outside the freight office, I asked every five minutes or so if a dog was on board. I called Deanne on my cell phone to tell her that Devon had arrived. I called my wife, Paula, for reassurance; convinced that three dogs was at least one too many, she didn't offer much. I called my daughter at college. "He's almost here," I announced. She sighed a familiar sigh. "Call back and let me know what he's like."

A half-hour after touchdown—it was by now nine P.M.—I saw two baggage handlers pulling a large blue dog crate, dragging and bumping it noisily across the tiled floor. The plastic container was enormous, with air holes along the sides, and a metal grill over the front opening. An envelope taped on top held the dog's travel and AKC papers. A blanket, the only vestige of his former life, was scrunched up against the door, along with an empty bowl, and shredded bits of newspaper lined the bottom.

I couldn't see much through the front grill, just flashes of black and white that seemed to circle frantically, like a pinwheel. He was throwing himself against the door and the sides. I winced at the loud bumping; he needed to get out of there.

They pulled the crate alongside me. "Hey, Devon," I said to the plastic. No response.

I presented the required ID, signed the freight bill, and pulled the crate to a part of the baggage area where there was a bit of room.

Newark Airport, almost always bedlam, was worse than usual that night because of bad-weather delays all over the East. Luggage was piled everywhere; cops screamed at idling drivers through the open doors; skycaps yelled for business; and the loudspeaker rattled off one flight after another as the jets roared overhead. Thousands of people poured through the doors and along the concourses.

My van was parked a few hundred yards from the door. My plan was to reach into the crate and leash Devon, then walk him with one hand while I toted the crate in the other; we'd get away from this madness and save our bonding for the quieter, darker parking lot. Section 3A of the Terminal B short-term parking area didn't exactly conjure up pastoral scenes from James Herriot, but it would have to do.

Inside the crate, Devon was still pinwheeling. I'd yet to glimpse his face.

"Devon," I called. "Devon, I'm going to open the door, boy. It's going to be okay." I've always talked to my dogs, not because I imagine they understand my words, but so that they can pick up my tone or mood. It's almost a reflex.

The thumping and twirling stopped, and I saw a pair of wild, ink-dark eyes. They bespoke power and intensity, as well as terror. And no wonder. In the morning, home, in laid-back, sparsely populated Texas. Then to the airport, into a crate, onto a plane's cargo hold. Takeoffs and landings, not once but twice. Holed up in the dark. Hours in the air. Unloaded down a ramp, driven across the airport's dank runways, dragged across the floor of a tumultuous terminal, confronted with a large stranger calling his name.

I knelt, pulled up the latch on the crate, and the gate slammed open into my face. Before I could move, a blur shot past me and into the crowd, its force knocking me off my heels onto my back. Devon was out of sight before I could scramble to my feet. A flurry of shrieks and shouts behind me told which way he'd headed.

It took me, two baggage handlers, and three very unhappy Port Authority police officers nearly half an hour to track and corral Devon as he ricocheted through the jammed terminal, scaring travelers out of their wits as he dashed in panic. He had no bearings, no reference points or instincts but flight.

The PA officers were not dog lovers, it turned out. "Hey, he's a champion border collie," I pleaded as one got on his radio to alert Newark's animal-control team.

"We aren't dogcatchers," he said. But he wasn't totally unsympathetic either, and they agreed that we would try to restrain Devon before calling in the doggie SWAT unit. They warned, however, that they wouldn't be held responsible if he nipped some kid, or if an old woman got knocked over. "I've seen dogs a lot less excited than that one bite people," one muttered.

Any mishaps would be on my head. And the officer wasn't wrong. A panicked dog in a strange place could be dangerous. What if someone grabbed him? But the thought of Devon locked up in a shelter made my stomach drop. So we set off after him.

He sprinted from one baggage carousel to another, then back again. He seemed to be desperately looking for some running room, or perhaps a familiar sight. He couldn't find either.

Whenever we'd get close, he'd turn and bolt, vanishing into the crowds. My nightmare was that he'd dash out one of the doorways into the vast parking lots, which stretched out forever, bounded by teeming highways. Devon could easily get hit—or, if he made it through, he might disappear into the acres of meadows, refineries, truck bays, and warehouses that surround the airport. I shouted his name. It didn't slow him a whit.

Occasionally, he'd wheel back toward us. A few brave and sympathetic travelers even called out and reached for him, but he turned, barked, and snarled. Parents grabbed their kids. The cops had lost patience.

But eventually we seemed to have driven him more or less into a corner near a Hertz counter, a cop on either side behind me. I was out front, moving slowly toward him.

I knelt in front of him, leaving a few yards between us. It was my first good look at him. Devon was a beautiful creature, sleek and black with a needle nose, a narrow white blaze on his forehead, a white chest. He was skinny, his fur matted, and he was hunched over after hours in the crate. I could see pale stains along his face, probably from panicky spittle during the trip. His eyes were inexpressibly deep, enchanting, and sad.

He was panting heavily, spent and frightened, probably dehydrated. I had to get him under control, or he'd end up in a Port Authority kennel or, worse, loping along a highway.

Eye contact was critical with border collies. All the books said so; it was the way they dominated livestock. Perhaps Devon would respond. At the least, a moment's pause in his race might give me a chance to grab him. I could see him gauging the distance between me, the officers to my rear and a small crowd of people, whom I suspected were concerned dog types, forming a raggedy semicircle behind the police.

He was an obedience dog, supposedly. "Devon. Stay. Devon. Stay," I kept repeating, a quiet chant. "I'm your new friend. I'm the guy. It's okay now. It's okay. Stay. We're going to go home." I kept my voice soothing and even, hoping the repetition would calm him. I was panting, too, and sweating.

I pulled a dog biscuit out of my pants pocket. His darting eyes focused on me, then glanced at the biscuit. I put it on the ground and nudged it toward him. He ignored it, looking almost disdainful. Could I possibly think he could be bought off that cheaply? He seemed offended.

And I could see him calculating, calculating, calculating. Can I run for it? Can I get past this jerk and all these people? A baggage carousel sputtering into motion caught his eye for a moment. Was that a possible escape route? Then, as if he'd suddenly grown resigned, his posture relaxed a bit. Maybe he had figured out that the terminal led nowhere he wanted to go. I inched forward on my knees slowly, talking quietly, feeling like a hostage negotiator. This was now a major scene. My anxiety was enhanced by acute embarrassment.

"Stay," I said, raising my palm, firming my voice. "Stay, Devon. It's okay." He seemed mildly amused now, and began concentrating on me, taking me in, pondering my technique, tilting his head curiously as I gestured. He was definitely listening to me, sizing me up.

I got closer, close enough to reach behind his ear and scratch him gently. He let me. The cops began to back away. Then some kid shouted, and Devon started, looking wild again. But I scratched him again, and patted his shoulders. I felt for his collar and slipped the leash onto the metal ring. He didn't resist or run, he just kept staring at me.

The leash seemed to settle him down, as if he finally understood what he was supposed to do, which was to go with me. The officers, muttering, looked relieved and went off to do something more important. At least nobody had been bitten or hurt.

By now, a number of people in the crowd were murmuring about how beautiful Devon was, clucking sympathetically when I loudly announced that he'd come all the way from Texas, that this was his first time on a plane, the first time he'd met me. And he *was* beautiful, this dervish who weighed, I guessed, somewhere between forty and fifty pounds.

I held the leash on my left, and Devon walked along hesitantly as I pulled the crate behind us. He wanted nothing to do with it.

"Heel," I tried, to no particular effect. But he wasn't trying to escape. For the moment, I was all he had.

We walked outside past the rows and rows of cars until we

reached the van. At first he lurched one way, then the other, then settled into trotting along beside me, turning as I did, the mark of a trained dog. Maybe I just didn't know the right commands.

I unlocked the van's rear door, pushed in the huge crate, then came around to the side, still holding the leash. A powerful curiosity was taking over a bit from the terror. Devon was noticing everything, reacting to every sound, to the lights, buses, and people. His eyes seemed astonishingly expressive and alert.

I pulled out the jug and bowl and poured him some water. He slurped it up greedily. Then I crouched next to him on the pavement. It was a surreal encounter in the ugly yellow safety light, with cars pouring past us in a stream, but Devon didn't shy away. I handed him another biscuit, which he inhaled. Then two more.

I reached over slowly and scratched the top of his head; his ears came up for the first time. Every thirty seconds or so, a jet would blast overhead and Devon would shake a bit, but after two or three takeoffs, he got used to it.

"Devon, listen to me, pal," I said, trying again. "It's going to be okay." He gazed up at me, and at the sky above us, and looked utterly lost and defeated. I kept scratching him and handing over biscuits, which he kept eating. He was making up his mind about me, as I was about him.

"Look, we're going to get into the car now. We're going to go home," I told him. "I don't know what you've been through, but

I work at home, I'll stay with you, I'll give you lots of walks, lots of food, lots of patience. I'll take good care of you. Let's try it, okay?" I held out my hand, and he licked it, once, very gently.

I opened the door and Devon jumped up onto the front seat as if he'd done it a million times. I lowered the front window a bit—he stuck his nose out. Curiosity was my ally here; from inside the van, the airport was more fascinating than terrifying—though when we got to the parking-lot cashier's booth, he jumped onto the floor and hid.

Then he jumped back up, looking at me, then out the window. The wheels were turning: Who is this guy? What is this place? Where are we going?

"It's okay," I kept saying. "It's all right." Sometimes he appeared to believe me.

Fifteen minutes later, we pulled into my driveway. The Labs came lumbering over to the fence, tails wagging. Devon's head went down, his ears folded, and the three touched noses cautiously. Julius looked at me with regret and concern. Stanley, the slightly more dominant of the two, looked skeptical.

I decided to take Devon for a short walk before introducing him to Paula and the house. Partway down the block, he was walking alongside me so easily, his nose to the ground sniffing the pavement, that I relaxed a bit for the first time that night. My tree-lined suburban street seemed serene compared to Newark Airport.

An ill-advised reverie: with a sharp jerk of the leash from my hand, Devon was gone. I spun around in all directions and saw no trace of him—until I happened to glance at a passing minivan and saw him perched on the roof as it drove slowly down the street. I didn't believe it. I *couldn't* believe it. Dogs don't fly.

Brandishing a pooper-scooper in my right hand, I gave chase, shouting as I went, "Hey! Hey, stop! Stop, there's a dog on the car." My neighbors walking their terrier across the street paused in shock and stared.

The van slowed, a trusting act by a driver who'd probably looked in his rearview mirror to see what the tumult was about. God knows what he or she thought at the sight of a 230-pound man galumphing down the street, waving a strange device and screaming. The van began to speed up.

My God, I thought, how did he get up there?

I stopped and shouted as loudly as I ever have, "Devon, come! Now!" My voice wasn't pleading, but angry. Perhaps thirty yards down the street, he hopped off as nimbly as if the van were a small step stool and lighted on the sidewalk.

"Sit!" I screamed. He did, looking up at me in some bewilderment, perhaps wondering why I was making so much noise. Then he averted his face, as if in shame or fear that I would strike him. He remained absolutely still as I grabbed his leash, and we headed back to the house.

My dog year had begun.

Two

OCEANGOING LABS

Watching the denouement of this drama from behind the back-yard fence, Julius and Stanley looked puzzled.

They were beautiful dogs, big and statuesque and all snowy white with soulful dark eyes. Walking Devon back toward the house, still in shock over his van-surfing ("What were you doing?" I asked him over and over), it dawned on me that I now would experience both ends of the canine spectrum. Julius and Stanley were as peaceful, responsive, and easygoing as Devon was wild and anxious.

❖❖❖❖❖❖❖❖

When I think of the Labs now, I picture a clear warm summer day at the National Seashore on Cape Cod.

The waves crash along the sand, gulls squawk overhead,

small fishing boats and giant freighters glide along the horizon, and the tawny dunes glow as the sun lowers.

All along the beach, the shrinks and writers and financial-services people from Boston and New York lie sprawled beneath their tasteful beach umbrellas, keeping one eye on their kids, the other on the *Times Book Review* or a hardcover novel.

Although dogs are officially prohibited on the public beaches, people bring them at the end of the day, when most of the families and park rangers have left, the lifeguards have climbed down from their stands, the hot-dog vendor has driven away from the parking lot, and a breeze comes up off the water.

The arriving dogs are usually good-natured, well-bred and trained, easy around people—the kind of dogs you want to bring along on your vacation and can take to a public beach without worry.

None of these dogs are more stately than mine. None have sweeter dispositions or look grander lying on the sand, as their ancestors did so faithfully generations ago, after hauling fish and nets up and down the shores of Newfoundland (though not the shores of Labrador: some English guy, for reasons of his own, changed the name of the breed).

If you walked down this beach and gazed admiringly at Julius and Stanley, as so many people did each summer, you would expect to see them, at any moment, bound down toward the water, plunge into the big waves, and swim halfway to Europe without working up much of a sweat.

You would wait a long time.

For me, this lovely scene is perenially bittersweet. Paula and I have been coming to this beach nearly our whole lives, long before we were married. We have always treasured time together with our daughter at the onset of twilight, the dunes turning shadowy, the quiet deepening, the cries of the gulls more haunting.

But this is also the hour of the nearly mythic oceangoing Labs, an annual humiliation, a sore point, an unflattering window into my insecure male vanity and misplaced expectations.

They materialize suddenly, big black and chocolate retrievers with sleek fur and barrel chests, conscious of their rugged Canadian heritage, casually arrogant. They head for the water, their owners nearby, equally sleek and cool, smug in their assurance that their dogs will soon be doing what nature meant them to do—plowing into the water, bringing something back.

Which is exactly what happens. The Labs canter, like mustangs on a prairie, right into the sometimes huge and powerful waves. Strong and fearless, they paddle out unhesitatingly toward their target, then return toting balls or sticks, sometimes a piece of driftwood. They emerge, shake off the water, and refocus, ready to take the plunge again and again. They don't play with or even notice other dogs or people, their eager eyes fixed on their owners and masters, to see in which direction they'll toss the prize.

This is serious stuff, the outcome of generations of careful breeding, a testament to the instincts and fidelity and courage of the working dog.

Julius and Stanley are watching the dogs as intently as I am, fascinated by these exotic creatures. I once imagined the sight might reawaken some dormant DNA in my dogs, trigger ancient instincts. Nope. Mostly, they seem to enjoy the show, like ticket-holders at a circus, enthralled by the spectacle but never dreaming of climbing into the ring.

Here at the ocean's edge, one is reminded of the origins of these particular working dogs. There is something beautiful about what they do, about their concentration and determination and the bond they have with their owners. It's one of the happy partnerships in the long, often sad, history of humans and animals.

Heavy surf or strong currents hardly seem to matter. The dogs tear through the waves undaunted, sometimes taking a wallop but always returning with their quarry. They can do this forever, it seems.

Their owners are proud and pleased. This is why you have a dog like this, after all, not only to have a pet, but to glory in the pride and heritage of the breed, to conjure a time when the relationship between people and dogs was essential, a matter vital to work, to life itself.

This has not been my experience with my Labs, even though their lineage dates to England and includes a slew of awards and decorations, and their long pedigrees hang framed on my office wall. I, too, have dreamed of standing at the beach, throwing a ball or stick for an oceangoing Lab. Instead, day after day, summer after summer, I sit with my wife and daughter and Julius and Stanley, observing the scene on either side of me.

Julius tried the ocean once, when he was little more than a puppy, inserting a paw like an old lady visiting Miami Beach. He looked disturbed. Too cold, too rocky.

Besides, as the sneering local vet told me when I subsequently carried Julius into his office with cracked and bleeding paws, he was delicate, probably allergic. The beach sand irritated his sensitive paw pads; the salt water stung them. I'd taken Julius on a hike through the Provincetown dunes once, and he ended up limping so badly I had to carry him back the last quarter-mile. He weighed more than eighty pounds at the time, and the rescue nearly killed us both.

Maybe booties would be in order, said the vet, practically smirking. There was no way, I replied frostily, that my yellow Lab was going to the beach in booties. If Julius's retrieving skills were rusty, his dignity was profound. There was mine to consider, too.

I don't even want to think about how many water toys I bought, how often I stood pleading with Julius to fetch while he wagged his tail and gazed at me ruefully. On occasion, I'd waded in after a toy or ball myself, hoping to serve as a role model. "Good boy," my daughter cheered as I emerged with the ball; she was going through her highly ironic phase. But none of this helped. Julius will go in up to his ankles sometimes, looking uneasy, and I know he's doing it for me, to salvage my pride.

Otherwise, he seems to have no interest. He doesn't chase balls. He just doesn't. But so what? I honor him for his own considerable gifts. Would these other dogs sit by my feet for hours at a stretch while I clack away at my computer?

Stanley offers some hope. An indefatigable ball-chaser, he loves to swim—but only in a lake or pond, please. No big waves. He's happy to wade into the surf, but at the first crash of a breaker, he turns on his heels, heads back to shore, and goes to sleep. Oceangoing Labs are diving and plunging all around him; he is not impressed. And when you think about it, they do look a little silly, like trained seals at aquarium shows. Where's the great tradition in chasing a floating stick?

Sometimes I take the boys to the bayside beach, where the water's warmer and the waves are mere ripples. Stanley will swim out, under these conditions, to fetch his retriever toy. I cheer him on. Julius watches.

They are incomparably regal, though. The casual observer

might think that they were merely resting between missions. Some passersby remark that my dogs must be superbly trained to sit on the beach like that despite all the temptations, to resist leaping into the water. Thanks, I say. Yes, they are very disciplined.

Well, they have other gifts. Kids come over to meet them, pat them, climb all over their furry bodies. My dogs are unfailingly friendly, gracious, affectionate. Parents seek Julius and Stanley out to show their three-year-olds that they don't have to be afraid of dogs. Maybe back in England or Canada the task of this particular strain of Labradors was to hang around with the royal kids while other, inferior dogs were sent out in search of game.

So what we do, mostly, is sit for hours. I read a book and stare out to sea. Whenever I reach a hand out to either side, a dog's square head is there for scratching, a dog's tongue gives me a lick. Julius and Stanley watch empathically as their cousins wear themselves out. My dogs are deeply spiritual beings, content to gaze at skittering sandpipers and ponder the state of the universe. They have no need to race around, no matter what their ancestors did. Times change.

❖❖❖❖❖❖❖❖❖

I fretted for weeks about the impact of a third dog on these two. Really agonized, mostly because I could hardly find anybody—

breeders, our dog trainer, my wife, the neighbors—who thought it was a good idea.

Two dogs are a pair, I'd read; three make a pack. The third can throw off the entire dynamic, setting up rivalries for dominance, food, and affection, causing anxiety or even aggression. Not to mention the practical concerns of caring for three dogs in a bustling New Jersey suburb: three would be harder to walk and clean up after, would run up the vet bills, would tear up the yard and bring more smells and hair into our already ratty house.

Julius would have no problem with an added dog, I knew, because Julius had no problem with anything. Stanley was a tad more assertive, and might cling to his number-two spot in the pack. He never bothered other dogs, but he wasn't crazy about them, either. He had bonded deeply with Julius, the only dog—apart from his sister Sally, who lived two blocks away—for whom he'd ever shown much affection.

But when it came to people, they were matchless. Julius was my soulmate. His stability and loyalty were anchors for a restless and volatile personality like mine. I smiled every time I looked at him.

Stanley was a mischievous playmate. We wrestled and played tug-of-war with rope toys. Over time, he'd developed a singular passion for ball-chasing and retrieving, and my tolerant neighbors never complained about his bounding across their lawns in pursuit on our daily outings.

I'm only mildly embarrassed to confide that the three of us had a game we especially loved: I'd sneak off into a corner of the basement or a bedroom closet, hide, and utter a single bark—a challenge for them to find me, hunting dogs that they are. The two of them would scour the house, sniffing, barking, rushing from room to room. Stanley was invariably the one who'd track me down—he moved faster than Julius—and there was much rejoicing with biscuits for all. Well, for two of us.

Other dogs grasped their gentleness and rarely challenged them. If they did, my dogs would back off, puzzled and eager to stay out of trouble. Julius, for one, would never expend the kind of energy it took to get into a fight.

When a kid came near, even a toddler, both dogs would sit down, tails wagging, and let the child approach, then gently lean over to give him or her a lick. In warm weather especially, it sometimes took a long time to circumnavigate our block, as both adults and children came out of their houses to say good morning, offer treats and pats, or just tag along. The FedEx man and the garbage-truck drivers were their pals.

They were either very wise or fairly dumb, I often thought, but the end result was the same: neither dog wished any creature harm, or ever hurt another living thing.

So why bring an emotionally battered border collie with high energy and low self-esteem into this perfect mix?

❖❖❖❖❖❖›❖❖

Almost everyone I knew asked me that question. Why import this strange dog all the way from Texas when I had two dogs I dearly loved, and who were settled into such a comfortable routine? Why one of the most high-strung and unstable breeds? Why go through all the training, expense, and disruption?

I have a history of doing things that aren't particularly smart—buying a run-down cabin in upstate New York, switching jobs, and even careers. I guess I'm a bit unstable and high-strung myself.

Maybe that's because I fear stasis, when the body is still vital but the mind sets like cement. Whenever I hear people clucking about the decline of civilization, what's wrong with young people, how vulgar popular culture is, how confusing and frightening they find the Internet, alarms go off. I know I'm around somebody whose hinges are rusting. Death will be bad enough, but for me, this early harbinger is more fearsome, because a part of one's spirit and openness and ability to learn and grow disappears. That's one possible explanation for this new adventure.

Here's another: my own family life had been complex and painful. I longed for someone who would come along and take care of me and my sister. Maybe I wanted the chance to do that for a creature like Devon, to be the benefactor who came along and took faithful care of him.

Another thought: having a child had been the central, most rewarding experience of my life. I loved being a father and was proud of the kind of father I usually was, mostly because I have such a great kid. Now that she's gone off to college, I don't really miss being a full-time dad, although I do miss her. But I'm not finished with nurturing yet, with raising and caring for living things. I didn't get to raise as many kids as I'd wanted.

Julius and Stanley had taught me that I'm good at this dog thing. I can raise and train and love dogs. They're not kids, but they, too, need clear, firm direction. I feel responsible for meeting their needs, while also making clear to them what is expected, what their end of the contract is.

It seems to me that people should develop and deepen the skills they have, even if they come later in life. If I had found something I did well and could get better at, why not take it seriously and, in the process, give one needy creature the loving sanctuary all creatures deserve?

Politics are abstract to me. I can't relate to liberals or conservatives. Dogs live on a scale that I can comprehend; their lives are an outcome I can affect. They make me happy, satisfy me deeply, anchor me in an elemental way. Sometimes it's hard for me to trust people, or to find people I can come to trust. I trust my dogs, though. They would do anything for me, and I for them. That's a powerful relationship, no matter what the species.

❖❖❖ ❖ ❖❖❖❖❖

It took a year after my golden retriever, Clarence, died young from kidney disease before I decided I was ready for another dog. At the time, I'd recently abandoned a journalism career to write at home. It was lonely at times in my basement office, and when I got stuck on a chapter or an idea, I had a habit of walking through the neighborhood to sort things out. Frequently stymied, I ended up walking three or four times a day. What dog wouldn't benefit from that, and from day-long companionship?

I'd bought Clarence in exactly the wrong, if all too common, way: eager to bring home a puppy for my toddler daughter, I'd stopped at a suburban pet store, mostly because it misleadingly had "American Kennel Club" in its name.

This was a lazy and risky approach. A dog enters your family for years, interacts with your spouse, children, and neighbors, lives in your house, becomes a constant presence. Yet few people—myself then included—seem willing to do the homework to make the right choices. Dogs bought from such stores are often inbred, produced in puppy mills, their health, background, and temperament all unknowable.

But golden retriever puppies are adorable, and even though I knew better, I wanted a dog, and this one was in my arms, licking my face and my daughter's. Once a kid gets his or her hands on a puppy, it's the rare parent who can dispatch it back into its cage and walk away.

Clarence was a great dog in many ways, but he had a raft of health and temperament problems. He was touchy around young children and strangers, had a bevy of allergies, and he died too young.

None of these difficulties kept me from nearly driving my car into a tree on the way home from the vet after he was put down.

The next time, reading books, talking to experts, taking advantage of those new tools the Internet and the World Wide Web, I had the chance to think through my decision more deliberately.

In my Boomerville town, big dogs were definitely in style, and a few stayed locked up in houses all day while everybody was at work and school. Hunting dogs were special favorites, because they are bred for patience and spending time with people, and because they are often beautiful. It was sometimes an unfortunate formula: the fewer people around, the bigger and more powerful the dog. People wanted a pet, but many were too pressed or eager for a puppy to focus long on the reality that big dogs need exercise, not to mention disciplined, labor-intensive, time-consuming training.

For the noblest of reasons, it had also become popular—and

immensely rewarding—to go to the local pound and bring home stray and abandoned animals. Many were lovely, companionable dogs, but some were mixed breeds unsuitable for suburban families, tense and unpredictable around other animals, kids, even their owners. This can also be true of purebred dogs, some of whom suffer from overbreeding and don't live up to their TV commercial images.

I wanted a dog with the right temperament and instincts for me, a dog I could get close to, have an affectionate but respectful relationship with. I'd do the work on my end, but I wanted to make sure that I had a dog that could carry his part of the bargain. That meant a breeder who knew me, knew his dogs, and could match us up; a person who'd be there if there were problems. So I started doing research.

I wound up a half-hour's drive north. The breeders—a vet and his wife—made an appointment to meet me. Before I could see a single dog, they sat me down in their living room and grilled me. I'd brought my daughter Emma along, but Paula was busy. Where was my wife, they wanted to know. (She was working.) Did she want a dog, too? (Sure, as long as I handled ninety percent of the feeding, walking, training, and grooming.) How many kids were at home? Had I had a dog before, and if so, what problems had I encountered? What was my lifestyle like? Did I believe in training? Neutering?

The couple obviously liked the fact that I worked at home,

liked to walk, and had a fenced yard. Even more, they liked my determination to train a new dog thoroughly. So they brought four-month-old Julius up from the kennel. He was delighted to make our acquaintance, licked me and Emma repeatedly, and when I took him in my arms, he fell asleep, his body cradled upside down, his head lolling. He came home with us.

A professional trainer named Ralph Fabbo—so calmly authorative that the freakiest, most out-of-control dogs would sometimes wet the floor when he appeared at their front doors—came to my house an hour each week for two months. He'd trained Clarence, and I needed no more convincing about the value of training after that. Julius became one of his very best students.

Stanley followed after Jules was firmly settled in the family, housebroken, and ready to help mentor a new puppy. They were swell guys almost from the start, though Stanley, in his puppy-hood, did gnaw the fringe off an area rug.

Under Ralph's direction, I'd spent many hours teaching Julius and Stanley to stay away from the street, to sit, stay, come, "leave it" (essential for hunting dogs, with their delight in scarfing down revolting things). They followed all these commands, quickly and without complaint. Their tails were always wagging.

◆◆◆◆◆◆◆◆◆

Their tails were wagging now, as Devon and I walked back to the house, and I opened the gate to the yard. The airport scene and van-jump were both jarringly fresh in my mind, but Devon seemed calmer now, his curiosity taking over. I thought he might be more relaxed about interacting with the Labs if he had some running room, so I let him off the leash.

Julius and Stanley looked still and alert, aware that something important had happened. They may also have sensed my tension. The fur along Stanley's spine stood up. Julius just came over and licked me, ignoring Devon completely. The three didn't have much to do with one another. There was no overt hostility, just lots of circling and sniffing.

When I opened the door to the house, the Labs lumbered up the stairs. Devon, however, leaped right over Stanley and took the steps in two hops. He raced into the living room, pivoted sharply—the Labs were staring at him in astonishment—then dashed into the kitchen, where he jumped onto the kitchen table, then off again, all before I could open my mouth.

It was like watching speeded-up film, all action.

Three

OLD HEMP AND OLD KEP

*D*evon *was a mess. His hair was matted and knotted, and* underneath the tangle, he was skinny as a chicken. His eyes indicated near-perpetual panic as he took in every sight and sound. His nails were long and sharp. His breath was foul, and since dog breath mints failed to solve the problem, I soon tried cleaning his teeth with treated wipes, then later with a special antiplaque dog toothbrush. He was not appreciative.

He was a split personality, fiercely proud and willful, but at the same time lonely and defeated, with a sense of anxious despair about him. His eyes were sometimes deep and mournful wells.

Somehow, in the intense, high-expectation world of the border collie, a breed that imposes rigorous standards on itself, he had failed. I would never really know what happened, but he didn't seem to have been loved, or to have succeeded in his obedience work. He was ultimately fired and dumped, a triple catastrophe that had to be crushing to such a dog, one bred for centuries to attach to a single person and energetically undertake important tasks.

He didn't appear physically abused so much as neglected and drained, like an employee who'd been laid off three times in one year and couldn't get a job interview. Yet, certain objects—brooms, flyswatters, sticks—would spark terror. He'd shake and hide in a corner.

No, I wasn't reading too much into this, Deanne counseled during one of our extended phone consultations. She hadn't had Devon back for long, and he mostly had stayed out back in her fenced-in fields with a score of other dogs day and night, so most of the problems I was having didn't show themselves. But she'd seen some of the same behavior; that's why she'd worked so hard to find him a new home.

Long after having sold him, Deanne told me, she ran into him one day at a competition where he was entered in the obedience trials. He'd left her proud and spirited, but now he appeared broken and discouraged. She was worried about him.

"He just looked unhappy," she said. "His ears were down. His tail was down. I kept asking myself, 'Why would his ears be down?' " This was no minor matter.

Somehow, she urged, I had to persuade Devon that I loved him and would stick with him, and at the same time—even more difficult since he was ferociously strong-willed—convince him to accept my authority without further damaging his psyche. I also had to train him to live compatibly in New Jersey with the other members of the household, human and canine. I feared this was way over my head.

That first night in our house, he lapped up bowls of water. He raced frantically, still panting, from room to room, sticking his head in Paula's lap, then in mine, then rushing to sniff the dogs. He jumped up on sofas and chairs, then off again, dashed upstairs and back down.

Julius and Stanley sat mute and astonished, their heads swiveling as Devon whizzed back and forth, a juiced-up, perpetual-motion machine. I wondered if he'd gone mad. The border collie books were filled with horror stories of these energetic dogs going insane with nothing to do.

He rattled me. He simply wouldn't light anywhere. He picked up rawhide strips and chewbones, then put them down. He created a circuit: to the back door, then to the front, to his food bowl, then the water bowl, then back to the living room, then around again. But he was always circling back to check on my whereabouts. He didn't have many fixed points, but I was becoming one of them.

Okay, we'd try a walk, all together. I put Devon on a leash and took him out with Julius and Stanley. Still wary and a bit confused, they walked ahead while Devon raced in circles around me, dodging left, then right, tangling my legs in the leash. Sometimes he'd walk calmly for a bit, then appear incapable of proceeding five feet in a straight line. For an obedience competitor, he seemed to have spent very little time walking on a leash.

Exhausted, we all went upstairs to bed. Expecting a night of frenzied pacing, I thought about having him sleep in a wire crate, but just the sight of it seemed to terrify him.

Julius and Stanley went to their dog beds, and I came over to pat each of them reassuringly. Julius wore his most reproachful look. Stanley seemed to be pretending that Devon wasn't there, perhaps in the hopes he would disappear. When Devon came too near him, Stanley let out a quiet growl, something truly out of character.

Still, the Labs always kept their priorities straight. Just as would have happened if I'd brought a mountain lion into the bedroom, both were soon on their L.L. Bean cedar beds, snoring.

Not Devon. He came over to my bedside and seemed to be awaiting instructions. I said, "Devon, down," and he dropped to the floor. But neither he nor I slept much that night. Between fitful snoozes, I watched him, and he watched me watching him. All night, I saw those deep black eyes.

They never closed, and never left my face.

I suddenly had some serious logistical problems. I couldn't walk three dogs, not if one of them was Devon. He needed lots of exercise but I didn't have time to walk the Labs and him separately each time. No ready solutions came to mind, other than training Devon to walk off-leash. After the first night, that seemed dangerous.

My Labs had been trained to walk off-leash since they were puppies, and had no interest in pursuing anything but a sunny spot in the backyard, while Devon was two years old and had no measurable attention span. What he did have was a powerful chasing and herding instinct.

He was so much more frantic and unsettled than I'd expected, a mixture of curiosity and stubborness. He was fearful and often anxious, but not so afraid that he was necessarily obedient or anxious to please. I was quietly ticked at Deanne. Why would she think this wild thing and I would make a perfect match? Why hadn't she told me what a mess he was?

I wanted Julius and Stanley to maintain as much of their normal routine as possible. The last thing I needed was for them to feel unsettled, and I had promised myself that if they showed prolonged signs of being disturbed or unhappy, Devon would have to go. I owed them at least that much.

So the next morning, I let the three dogs out into the backyard, then carefully latched the gate, leaving Devon in the yard for a while as I walked the Labs. I'd gotten no farther than the corner when I sensed something behind us and turned to see Devon sitting on the sidewalk, watching me.

Had I left the gate open? No, it was still latched. How had this dog gotten out? Jumped the fence? There wasn't time to dig underneath it.

I reached for his collar; he bolted. Outside of a greyhound track, I'd never seen a dog move so fast. Devon rocketed away across the intersection of the next street and hurtled toward the elementary school on the next block.

Shooing Julius and Stanley into the yard—wide-eyed, they both sat down to watch—I tore after Devon with a leash in one hand and my pooper-scooper in the other. I heard horns and shouts as I neared the school, wheezing and sweaty.

A school bus had halted just before the school, and Devon was crouched in herding position in front of it, barking furiously, nipping at the tires, giving the bus the evil eye. He was trying to herd it. "No, no," I yelled. "It's not a sheep. It's not a sheep!" Even as the words left my mouth, I was aware that this was a curious thing to be shouting. But no one was paying attention anyway, least of all the dog.

The bus driver was shouting and hitting the horn. Parents were yelling. Devon, fixated on the tires, remained undeterred.

This dog and I had one slim chance of emerging from this

without a court date: we had to get the hell out of there as speedily as we'd arrived.

I ran up to him, screaming, "Stay!" He kept barking furiously. I leaned over and smacked him on the butt to get his attention; startled, he stopped, but looked at me with excitement and joy, inviting me to join in. It was the happiest I'd seen him by far; his ears were up at last. It took him a moment to realize that I was not as happy as he was.

I snapped on the leash and dragged him away, yelling apologies to the driver, kids, and bystanders. "He's a sheepdog," I tried to explain. "Like in *Babe*. He was working. He thought he was after a big, fat, yellow sheep." I smiled as warmly and unthreateningly as I could.

We walked away with exaggerated casualness, rounded a corner, and took refuge in a small park. Furious, I was yanking him along roughly, then was instantly sorry as he turned jumpy and scared all over again. I sat down on a bench; Devon sat down across from me, panting, looking guilty. His ears were down. He had nearly been killed several times on this brief adventure.

"Devon," I said wearily. "What the hell were you doing? You can't do that. You can't herd school buses. You can't run off like that. You can't run away."

He climbed onto the bench and collapsed in my lap, leaning up to lick my face. I hugged him. His tail started wagging for almost the first time since we'd met.

I wanted to assure him that I would never abandon him, but I stopped myself. I didn't know if that was true, not yet. If I made that promise, I had to mean it, because this dog would know.

Dogs don't understand our conversations (although with Devon, I couldn't be sure), but they definitely know whether you're on their side or not. I wanted somehow to let Devon know that I cared about him. I wanted him to forgive the smack on the behind. No dog owner is a saint, and anybody can lose his temper in a difficult spot, especially when safety is involved. And I had a long and deep relationship with impatience. But apart from the obvious, the problem with hitting or screaming at dogs all the time is that it doesn't work; they usually just become more fearful and anxious. It's not only cowardly but ineffective. Over the next few months, I was to learn a lot of things about myself, patience, and dogs, mostly that I didn't know as much as I thought about how to train them properly.

Still, I'd just had another sobering demonstration of the power and impulsiveness of his instincts. If this was going to work, I had to get through to Devon in some way that left us both alive.

For the next few days, every time I drove off and left him in the yard—the one time I left him alone in the house, he jumped on a table and knocked the phone and answering machine onto the floor—I would glance in my rearview mirror to see him sitting calmly outside the latched gate. I couldn't figure it out.

I tried to trick him. I left him in the backyard, got into my car, drove around to the front of the house, ran in through the front door, and raced to the windows in the rear of the house to see if I could catch him trying to escape. No good: he was sitting in the yard, peering at my face in the window.

Sighing, I went back outside, got into my car, drove down the block, then several minutes later headed back to the house on foot, sneaking in as quietly as I could manage.

My yard is enclosed by a whitewashed picket fence. Through the window, I saw Devon in the yard, racing to each slat, inserting his needle nose in the spaces between. When he found a loose slat, he wiggled his nose furiously, pushing the wood to one side. He squeezed through the narrow opening and then—here's the scary part—turned around and pushed the slat back into position.

Then he ran onto the sidewalk and sat down, watching for my car, leaving no evidence of his escape route. Devon understood the concept of covering his tracks.

I ran out the back door yelling, a dumb strategy. If you don't catch dogs in the act of wrongdoing—almost at the exact moment of transgression—then scolding only confuses them. They have no idea what you're shouting about. But a dog who's smart enough to move slats might be smart enough, I thought, to grasp that I was angry. Could I convey to him that this was a life-and-death issue, that a dog couldn't be loose on the busy streets of northern New Jersey and survive for long? That there was danger to others as well, to older people and kids and dog-phobic people, to drivers who might slam on their brakes and cause accidents if they saw a dog running through the neighborhood? That this, more than any other single thing, could put him on a plane back to Texas?

Devon looked at me defiantly, with a soon-to-be-familiar challenge: *You leave me, you'll pay every time.*

Devon wanted to be loved, yet he also had a powerful independent streak. Battered though he might have been, it hadn't left him submissive in any normal canine sense.

His escape sent me back to Janet Larson's book, which included a description, written in 1600, of the perfect shepherd's dog: "He ought to be gentle to his own household, savage to those outside it, and not to be taken in by caresses. . . . He should be black in his coat in order to appear more fearful to sheep thieves in the daylight and being the same shade as night itself, to be able to make his way unseen by the enemies and thieves." What was a backyard fence to a dog like that?

All contemporary border collies trace their lineage back to two dogs, says Larson. "Old Hemp," a champion of the late 1800s, was a sensation. He began hitting the sheepdog trials when he was a year old, Larson recounts, and he remained unbeaten for his entire life, a record unequaled by any other dog.

Old Hemp was tough on sheep, nor was he so easygoing where people were concerned, exhibiting certain ancient border collie traits—a rough nature and a strong dislike of strangers.

But the other ancestor of the breed, "Old Kep," raised in the early 1900s by a breeder named James Scott, had a kindlier disposition. He's credited with improving the temperament of the breed—at least some members thereof.

"Today," writes Larson, "there is not a border collie alive that does not carry the blood of these two great dogs."

How might Old Hemp have reacted to a middle-aged man with a pooper-scooper telling him to stay in the yard? Whenever Devon acted up, I began invoking the ancient names. What would Old Kep do? If those two were in his bloodline, maybe he'd get the message.

Meanwhile, I nailed the loose fence slat shut. Over the next few days, Devon found another loose one, then another, then half a dozen. I nailed them all in place, while the Labs dozed in the backyard and he watched every single hammer blow on every single nail. "Fuck you," I said as I hammered. "You are not getting out of this yard."

Devon cocked his head whenever I spoke directly to him. Just natural dog behavior for this breed, I knew, but I had the sometimes creepy certainty that he was listening carefully. I also took note of the fact that I was babbling to a dog.

Later that day, I returned from walking Julius and Stanley and found Devon waiting for me on the front lawn. He had, I later saw, learned to open the porch screen door with his left paw.

❖❖❖ ❖❖❖❖❖❖

It dawned on me slowly that Devon and I had entered upon an epic and intensely personal conflict, a contest of wills and wile made all the more interesting by the fact that only one of the principals understood just how brutal and protracted it was going to be. Devon became bored with trying all the slats, so he tunneled underneath the fence. He could produce amazingly large holes in what seemed like seconds.

When I left him inside, I'd find other signals that he was unimpressed with my authority: cabinets opened, shoes piled up neatly, loaves of bread still in their wrappings taken upstairs and deposited on the bed. None of these things was damaged, just intended as a message: Every time I left him, I would pay. It was his refrain, his work.

Once or twice, just to let me know he could, he simply hopped right over the fence as I left and was sitting calmly on the sidewalk when I returned. I know this only because a neighbor was watching and ratted him out.

Over the next few weeks, I came to realize, in my bovine way—I am not descended from Old Hemp—that Devon could get out of the yard any time he really wanted to, in a variety of known and as-yet-unexplored ways. The only way he would stop was if he wanted to.

He was as determined a rebel as Robert E. Lee, as iron-willed. But Lee faced a powerful army, and had eventually surrendered. I wasn't sure that Devon, who faced only me, ever would.

Four

MANIC PANIC

If you were sketching a walk with Julius and Stanley, you'd draw two long straight lines hewing more or less to the sidewalk. One for me, as I ambled along with my hands in my pockets, mulling over an article or book I was writing. One for Julius, veering off just a bit for extended sniffs of bushes, roots, or other mysterious lures; he liked to take his time. A third line, Stanley's, would have spikes off to the right, indicating joyous dashes after the blue ball he always wanted me to toss, but between fetches, he, too, stuck to the sidewalk.

A sketch of Devon's walk would resemble the diagram of a complicated NFL play, with all sorts of crazy circles and arrows shooting out in every direction. He'd trot a few feet ahead, then circle me a couple of times before heading off the other way. He turned into every driveway and walkway to investigate, and loped around every bush, perhaps in search of stray sheep. He never paced alongside me, but instead darted ahead and returned in long loops. At first I was constantly shouting at him to stop or come. But I soon realized that he was herding me, and would always keep me in sight. He never strayed too far; he also never stopped moving, panting, rushing, lunging.

Equal parts manic and panic, Devon had the look in his eyes you see in movies when a horse comes across a rattlesnake: lots of white.

My hastily improvised strategy—try to establish a bond so I could undertake real training—involved a brush. One of my books suggested that border collies loved to be brushed.

One morning, with the Labs safely ensconced in the yard chewing on peanut butter–flavored rawhide, Devon and I headed out to a nearby park. We found a bench in a secluded corner—no dogs, kids, cars, or vans to distract us—and I offered him a few biscuits, which he sniffed and ignored. Then I sat down and, pulling a metal-toothed brush from my jacket pocket, gave him a slow and gentle once-over. As I leaned over and brushed him in long strokes, down his back, along his haunches, down his chest, he grew nearly relaxed. His tail swished slowly back and forth. There was a whiff of contentment about him for the first time. He liked feeling cared for.

It was revealing evidence that he was not entirely a wild

creature, but a sweetie, a cream puff beneath the jangled nerves and inexhaustible energy. After the first couple of days, he'd put his paws up on my shoulders after we'd finished brushing, a kind of hug, and I'd hug him back. "It's okay, boy," I'd say over and over, as if repeating it might make him believe it. "It's okay now."

Pretty soon I could say, "Come on, Devon, let's go get brushed." He'd glance over at the brush, then dart to the back door, understanding exactly where we were going.

On the way to the park, I noticed, he didn't circle, chase, or herd. He walked right alongside me, immensely pleased with himself, perhaps because he'd found a perfect sap for an owner.

In these moments, we felt the first genuine stirrings of affection for each other. He knew I was going to take care of him; he appreciated it. I, who would have had fifteen kids if medical circumstances permitted (and if I'd married an heiress), loved caring for things.

Julius and Stanley now took care of themselves, pretty much. I had no more elementary-school car pools to pilot. But this guy Devon needed me, and I was ready to work hard at winning him back from the dark side.

I couldn't spend my days brushing him, but, inaugurating the next stage of my campaign, I began praising him extravagantly for just about everything: if he walked ten yards in a straight line, if he finished his own dog food and left the Labs' bowls alone, if he came when I called, if he just sat quietly looking gorgeous. "Good boy, Devon, good, good boy," became the mantra, repeated endlessly.

Though you really didn't have to say things two hundred times to a dog this smart, a couple of days of encouragement made a startling, visible difference. His ears stood up, his chest stood out. Initially so hunched and ratty, he seemed taller, his paintbrush tail held high.

His black coat took on a lustrous sheen after all that brushing. The first signs of mischievous glint occasionally appeared in his eyes. And he looked great. He was a magnificent dog, I was a bit surprised to discover, and when we walked, people began pulling over in their cars to admire him, as they often did with the Labs.

Perhaps Devon just never had what Julius and Stanley took for granted—attention, approval, and companionship. Maybe we'd made a start at trust.

❖❖❖ ❖❖❖❖ ❖

Border collies dislike nothing so much as enforced idleness. They need to come along, to see things and go places, chew stuff, run around, dig holes, keep a close eye on all comings and goings. They have intellects, and in the absence of something that interests them, they'll find unfortunate hobbies. Devon could already open cabinets and doors almost at will, and dig a bomb-sized crater in minutes. If I couldn't come up with tasks for him, he'd grow neurotic and destructive, and then my wife might, too.

Devon also had the powerful herding and chasing instinct he'd inherited from Old Hemp. When a truck or noisy car passed us on our walks, he'd bolt after it, pulling me so powerfully he nearly ripped the leash from my hand or pulled me over, half-strangling himself in the process. He seemed to love big, loud things in particular; a sanitation truck was irresistible.

It was a fine line to walk—training him while simultaneously building up his confidence. He wanted to work, but how to herd in suburban New Jersey? I couldn't let Devon chase anything that took his fancy.

Whenever he lunged after a car or truck on my street, I'd yell or throw the pooper-scooper on the sidewalk (dogs hate metallic noises, Ralph had taught me). I made a huge noise—"doing the bear," I called it. It was something I believed you had to do once in the life of every dog, and more than once with some. With my voice and body language, I was telling Devon that I was more powerful than he was, that there were forces on the planet greater than his need to herd.

Once or twice, I even whacked him on the butt. This was one of those dog battles you couldn't lose. I don't hit dogs, but with Devon, overcoming his attention-deficit disorder was a huge battle. Getting his acquiescence was another. His life depended on this, as well as his ability to stay with us and join our family.

There could be give-and-take on many of the issues we faced, but not on running into the street after cars and trucks. Otherwise, I'd have to call Deanne and send him back, or visit one of those border collie Web sites I'd been haunting to locate somebody with a pasture and a few sheep.

Beyond that, we had to establish an understanding. We could be great pals (he could already tell I would spoil him rotten) but ours wasn't an egalitarian relationship. As a Boomer parent in a child-centric town, I'd spent years watching people struggle to say no to their kids and their dogs.

But the foundation of a good relationship with any dog is a clear line of authority. They're pack animals. You have to help a dog understand exactly where he or she ranks in the pack, and the dog can never be number one. If you don't establish your dominance, you're not making life easier for the dog, you're condemning him to a life of confusion, disappointment, and destructive behavior.

That Devon was already two years old made things a lot harder. This was the border collie equivalent of peak adolescence, Deanne cautioned, under the best of circumstances a period of testing and tussling. Puppies can be taught how to behave from the beginning. Devon, who hadn't even been neutered until a few weeks before Deanne had shipped him east, had probably been trained to hone the very instincts I was trying to control, or at least channel.

I thought Julius and Stanley would both keel over in shock and horror at my noisy battles with this new arrival. Such outbursts had never been necessary with the Labs, and sometimes they couldn't distinguish my anger and frustration at Devon from disapproval of their own faultless behavior. Plus, they sensed my tension and frustration. When I shouted or threw a choke chain in Devon's direction (another metallic noise) they both dropped to the ground, their ears back, tails wagging, wondering how they'd screwed up. They were getting nervous; there was a lot of yelling, too much.

Fortunately, we came to an ingenious, if unorthdox, solution to the need-to-work problem.

The park where we went for brushing had a fence that ran parallel to a moderately busy street. We'd take up position about a hundred yards back from the fence. When a truck or car whizzed up, Devon would drop into the border collie herding crouch, tail down, eyes locked on me for some ancient command.

I didn't know exactly what signal cranked up Old Kep, but as a vehicle hoved into sight, I yelled, "Go get 'em, Dev." It was important to sound excited, I figured, or he wouldn't feel truly useful. The dog would shoot toward the fence like a rocket, then veer right to run parallel to the car or truck, keeping the fence between them.

The fence, a tall and sturdy chain-link, ran for a hundred

yards or so, and Devon would run to the very end, barking, then race back toward me in a long arc. He couldn't be deterred or distracted. He didn't want to stop, even when his tongue was dangling.

After half a dozen dashes, spit caked the fur around his mouth and his chest was heaving. But he was nearly grinning and afterwards was so calm that he seemed to enter a trancelike state. He even began dozing in the spring sun in the backyard for brief stretches, just like the Labs.

Drivers, city workers, commuters, kids, and other dog owners started wandering over to watch. Sometimes in the evening, we'd find a cluster of kids gathered to see "that dog that runs so fast." One kid dubbed him Speedy, and brought a stopwatch.

Julius and Stanley were happy to accompany us. They sniffed around, went over to lick whatever kids were at hand, received many pats, hugs, and plaudits, then stretched out to nap in the grass and feel the setting sun on their white backs. Stanley never saw the point of dashing around if there wasn't a ball to chase. Julius never saw the point at all.

But Devon got the idea quickly and loved it, as he did all chores. As long as he stayed safely behind a fence, he could chase and herd without threatening or endangering anyone, including himself. I began to understand how smart he was, too.

Devon instantly grasped that he could chase his prey here in the park but not anywhere else, and he stopped trying.

This "work" was a breakthrough. It strengthened the bond between us, as Devon turned to me for my dopey but effective signals. It permitted the release of a powerful, potentially explosive, energy. Herding, suburban style. It might not make the covers of the border collie magazines, or shows on the Discovery Channel, but we were making do.

Border collie breeders fret continually about over-domesticating these dogs, erasing the working abilities for which they've been so long prized. But maybe I didn't have to; maybe I could find a series of tasks that satisfied his instinctual needs, even without sheep.

But it was difficult to find the time and energy to sustain this rehab work. Devon had only been with us for a week, but I was exhausted, dog-walking four times as much and five times as fast as I had before he arrived. The equilibrium of my house, my Labs, and my work had been disrupted. We had a lot of training to do, and we hadn't even really begun. I wasn't yet sure that this dog truly belonged with us, or would be happy here, or that I was equal to the demands.

It had taken a couple of years for Devon to become a nervous wreck; how long would it take to reclaim him? Was it even really possible?

It was time to head for upstate New York, to my cabin, where dogs could indeed roam freely, where Julius had honed his Zen-like concentration to new levels, where Stanley could chase balls and toys right into lakes and streams with wild glee. We'd have male-bonding time together, the four of us.

Getting ready for the long drive, I put Devon in my ten-year-old Trooper and drove to the neighborhood shopping area for provisions: bread, milk, cash, a sandwich so I could eat lunch at a New York State Thruway rest stop without leaving the dogs in a hot car. Devon liked sticking his head out of the Trooper's window and watching the shoppers come and go.

He also, I discovered a couple of hours later, had carefully nosed his way into the paper bag on the front seat, somehow unwrapped the contents and extracted the ham from my sandwich, leaving the cheese and bread untouched.

Five

ON THE MOUNTAIN

The prescription called for some time off and emotional connections—between Devon and me, Devon and the Labs, Devon and the mountain. What we needed was trust and affection, both of which had to form before training would work. We also needed a place without cars, trucks, buses, or fences, a place where a border collie could relax and I wouldn't have to be screaming at him, where we could both catch our breath and take the measure of each other.

It wouldn't hurt, either, if it were a place already so ramshackle that the presence of a lively two-year-old border collie, two big yellow Labs that shed, and me could only improve it, and so remote that no amount of mayhem would be noticed.

That meant my shag-carpeted, weed-strangled, bug-and-mice-infested hideaway on the top of a mountain. The house was run-down, but the view was fit for royalty—the cabin looks out over a valley of farms and meadows that stretches all the way to Vermont's Green Mountains.

The mountain had a rich history for the Labs and me. Julius, Stanley, and I had retreated there for much of a brutal winter, had undergone a number of dramas and happy experiences there.

Dogs roved all over up there, along with all manner of other creatures. It would be the perfect place for Devon to get to know all of us and to chill a bit.

So I piled everybody into the Trooper, along with a new dog bed and sacks of chewbones and biscuits. On the drive north, I put the Labs in the rear section, where they slept during the entire four-hour trek. Devon took the backseat, where he paced furiously for two hours straight until I opened a rear window and he, delighted, popped his head out.

Dog owners are constantly—and for good reason—warned not to allow dogs to stick their heads out of windows while cars are speeding along; bugs and other debris can hit their faces and eyes and, in extreme circumstances, a car or truck passing too close can injure them.

Despite this sensible rule, there is nothing I find more pleasing than a dog peering out of a cruising car, the wind flattening his ears, a look of almost sensual contentment on his face. Maybe it conjures up ancestral memories of standing on a Welsh moor dotted with sheep.

Looking in my rearview mirror as we steamed up the Thruway, I caught sight of Devon's handsome head just outside the window, his nose toward the wind like the prow of an ice-breaker slicing through Arctic seas. He loved it.

My smile froze quickly when I heard frantic clawing behind me and learned how wise the anti-window rule was. In the mirror, I saw that Devon had lunged halfway through the narrow opening toward the trucks rumbling past in the other direction and was scrambling to get back inside. Steering with one hand, I reached behind me, grabbed his tail, and maneuvered him into the car, then found his collar and eased him back onto the seat. Heart pounding, I then closed the window for the remainder of the drive.

✦✦✦✦✦✦✦✦✦

I couldn't imagine the mountain without Julius and Stanley. They were as much a part of it as the view or the trees and streams. In a way, the mountain retreat had saved my life. As with Devon, I'd bought it over the mild objections of Paula, who pointed out that we were having enough trouble maintaining one decrepit house.

But as it turned out, I desperately needed that house and still do. A restless, anxious personality, I needed the peace. I was turning fifty then, struggling with my work, sending my adored daughter off to college, feeling trapped and worn in my New Jersey life. The Labs and I arrived in 1997 to rent and then buy the cabin, to fix it up a bit, to weather summer thunderstorms and winter blizzards, all of us blissfully unfamiliar with the outdoors.

I had arrived in midsummer and, with the help of some stalwart locals, scrambled to get it habitable for the winter. We encountered plumbing and wiring nightmares; mice, raccoons, and squirrels; mosquitoes, vicious flies, and other plagues.

From the first day, though, Julius found a spot right at the top of the mountain, just beyond the porch. He would bound out of the car, head for his spot, circle, and plop down. His head was immediately surrounded by clouds of flies, mosquitoes, and no-see-ums, the torturous little bugs that fly up your nose and into your eyes and ears, but he didn't seem to notice.

He was crazy about this vantage point. He could focus on Mount Equinox fifteen or twenty miles away, and stare hypnotically at the hawks circling the valley below the house. I think most of all he loved the fact that absolutely nothing was expected or required of him but to be.

Of the three of us, Julius was by far the most spiritual, reflective, at peace with himself and the world. He embodied the code and personality I wanted to possess but didn't: Think no ill, do no harm, spread love and happiness.

Down at the foot of the meadow a parade of wildlife passed by—rabbits, red foxes, raccoons. Julius watched them appreciatively. He was the Ferdinand of Labradors, never chasing any of his undomesticated colleagues. When deer bounded out of the woods fifteen feet away from him, he looked amazed. Sometimes the fur on his back stood up and he whoofed quietly, a sop to appearances. Usually, he just watched them graze.

It was upstate where Stanley learned to love chasing balls and to swim. I'd toss a ball down into the meadow and Stanley would roar off in pursuit, catch up with it, turn, and bound back up the hillside.

After fifteen minutes of this, especially in warm weather, he'd be spent, panting heavily. He'd drop the ball, settle next to Julius, and go to sleep. After a long bout of contemplative staring, Julius would doze off, too. He loved his spot, and I cleared away some of the brush and planted some grass seed so it would be more comfortable for him. I christened it Julius's Pew.

If I came out to sit, read, watch, or eat, Julius would amble over and sit next to me. Among his many gifts was a lack of intrusiveness. He knew how to be with you without bugging you. He was content to simply be there, a reassuring, comforting presence.

Stanley was more mischievous, a fun-loving dog, not a contemplative one. The great joy of his life was plowing into the Battenkill River or a nearby lake to chase his retriever toy—a floating rubber ball with a short length of nylon rope attached.

If he couldn't be an oceangoing Lab, he was prince of the ponds. I'd toss the water toy as far as I could, and Stanley would paddle out like a stately frigate. As he chugged along, you could see flashes of the Lab's amazing amphibian construction—head above the water, tail acting like a rudder, strong lungs powering the strokes, sleek, oily hair slicing through the water.

He would keep his eye on the floating ball, make a wide circle to come around behind it, chomp down on the yellow cord, and steam toward shore. He was undeterrable, resolute, and I was proud of him.

We did have some hair-raising aquatic and rural adventures, however.

There was the late-winter afternoon when Stanley ran out onto the frozen lake in pursuit of a ball and fell through the ice. He struggled to clamber out of the water but couldn't get any purchase with his front paws. After a couple of minutes of shouting encouragement, I saw that he was getting frenzied and tired. I was afraid he'd slip under and drown.

I couldn't watch. I pulled off my shoes, ran onto the ice, slid toward him on my stomach, calling out reassuringly—and fell through as well.

Fortunately, the water was shallow enough for me to stand in. I could pull Stanley out onto solid ice and climb out myself. But the half-mile back to the car was the longest of my life; I was sure we were seconds from frostbite.

That was less dramatic, though, than the time I brought the dogs to the Battenkill after a raging nor'easter to see the flooded river, surging at least a dozen feet over its banks. Stanley wanted, as always, to chase the ball, and I stupidly tossed it for him, not quite realizing how deep and fast the swollen river had become.

He dashed in, got caught in the unexpected current, and tangled in some vines and brush that would normally have been growing harmlessly on the bank. He was being pulled steadily out to midstream, where the water was churning. I plunged in up to my chest—the river was bitterly, icily, bone-crunchingly cold—slipped on the muddy bottom, and fell forward, tangled in the same undergrowth of uprooted roots and vines below the surface.

Given a chance to reflect calmly on this practice of submerging myself in frigid waters to rescue Stanley, I'm sure that like most half-bright people, I'd conclude that the risks were too high. But on the spot, I couldn't endure the sight of Stanley being pulled under, the innocent victim of his playful instincts and my thoughtlessness.

In the water, Stanley was struggling, looking frightened. I grabbed him, then found I couldn't move. My legs were quickly turning numb, and even a few feet from shore the torrent was alarmingly strong. Stanley was paddling to stay afloat but not, it seemed to me, very powerfully. I held him while trying to free my ensnared feet. I couldn't manage it.

The numbness was spreading, and it was nearly time to make a horrible decision—let him go or freeze. Maybe I'd let him go and I'd still freeze. I wondered what Paula and my friends would make of such a death. She'd probably know that it involved my doing something dumb with the dogs.

Was I really willing never to see my family again because of a yellow Lab? But I didn't let go.

While I frantically kicked to free myself and clung to Stanley, who was starting to panic, I felt a huge splash and a weight against my head and shoulders, followed by painful scratching and flailing. Julius had been watching from the shore and had jumped in, landing almost on top of me. It was the only time I'd ever seen him dive into water.

If his less-than-graceful landing on my head hurt, it also did the trick, knocking me clear of the vegetation. I was able to pull Stanley out of the current and toward the shore until, with a push, he could swim out onto the bank. Julius turned and swam out like a beaver himself. You fraud, I thought, you could swim all this time!

Up ahead, on a bridge a hundred or so yards downstream, normally high over the river but at this point only a few feet above its surface, I saw people pointing and waving. They were yelling, pantomiming phone calls—they were going to get help.

It was so bitterly cold that I ran up to the car. As the dogs shook themselves, I pulled off all my clothes and stood naked and shivering behind an unoccupied wood-frame building. Julius, still concerned, hovered worriedly. Stanley was coughing up water.

I had a duffel bag in the car—I had packed it for the drive home to New Jersey after our walk—and put on dry clothes and used my spare underwear to dry the dogs. I piled all the muddy, soggy garments on the floor of the Trooper, emptied the water and crud out of my hiking boots, let the dogs in the back, and took off, driving in my socks.

How could I possibly explain this to a cop, or a friend, or anybody? Would I confess that I'd thrown a ball into a flooded river to amuse my Labrador, then jumped in and nearly drowned trying to pull him out? It was too ridiculous.

Driving down the road, I passed a county sheriff's cruiser and a volunteer ambulance, lights flashing and sirens shrieking, racing in the opposite direction. Could they be coming for me? I didn't wait around to find out.

When we got home to New Jersey hours later—I was still shivering—Paula helped me unload and looked incredulously at the pile of filthy, soaked clothing.

"What on earth . . . ?" she asked. I just said I'd fallen. She didn't buy it; I refused to elaborate. She had her secrets, I had mine.

❖❖❖❖❖❖❖❖❖

Even before that, during our first summer weeks on the mountain, our little trio shared plenty of misadventures. We got caught outside in crackling thunderstorms. Our mountain road was sealed off during a forest fire and we spent much of one night huddled by the roadside below, waiting for the all clear.

One gorgeous afternoon, I went for a long walk with the boys along a supposedly abandoned railroad track. Midway across a rusty trestle bridge, forty feet above ground, we all heard a sudden whistle. We barely escaped with our skins.

Another afternoon, toward sunset, I got lost in the overgrown woods behind the cabin. I hoped Julius and Stanley would rescue me—"Take me home, boys!" I commanded—but they just looked at me mutely. They didn't want to sleep outside. When it grew darker, I gathered some leaves and twigs and made myself an extremely uncomfortable bed, thinking we'd have to spend the night outside. Instead, listening for road noise and walking toward it, we emerged—and I realized that we were never more than a few yards from the house.

One of these episodes didn't reach such a happy resolution. Walking our usual route on a midwinter morning, snow blowing horizontally into our faces, we headed down a steep incline into a field down the road. Ready to head back a little while later, I started to climb back up the incline, stumbled, and fell. Slippery ground, I figured, and tried again. And then again.

I don't know why it took me so long—denial, probably—to realize that my left leg wasn't working. It wouldn't respond; I couldn't put weight on it.

I had brought my cell phone—a safety precaution during

rural winters—and wondered if I should call my friend Jeff, who lived ten minutes away. But to say what? That I couldn't stand?

I've always taken my legs for granted. The sudden discovery that one of them wasn't functioning the way it had for a half-century was frightening.

I felt a warm nuzzle against my face. Julius put his great and beautiful head next to mine. I patted him, suddenly aware that I was near tears. What was happening to my body? I loved walking; it was my sport, my recreation, my way of being able to think things through.

Jules's sudden howl was chilling, a piercing, mournful keening that I'd never heard before. He pointed his head to the sky and wailed. Whatever was happening, he'd grasped its import. Stanley, alarmed, came running over to lick my face.

I managed to roll over onto my side and crawl to my feet, using the wire that anchored a utility pole for support. Julius walked by my side every step of the way back to the house.

I wear two braces now, one placed in my shoe, one strapped around my ankle. My tendon is shot, an orthopedist tells me, probably from an old and unnoticed injury, and the bones in my ankle have been collapsing for years. It hurts. But I keep walking and hiking, and when I fall, I hear Julius's mournful cry. He knew.

Most of the time, though, our days on the mountain were less eventful. In winter, we spent a lot of time in front of the big brick fireplace, trying to stay warm. Most summer nights were cool, and whenever I woke up, I found two big white Labs curled up in bed with me, sleeping peacefully. I rather liked the company and appreciated the warmth. Some mornings, we'd watch the sun come over the Green Mountains together, sitting outside in the dew, I with a steaming cup of coffee, the lads with an extra large lite biscuit, as a chorus of songbirds trilled.

Nearly every day we went for a hike together, usually through the Merck Forest in Vermont, a preserve we all treasured.

I'd find a log to sit on, take out a Thermos and sandwich and a supply of treats and rawhide, and we'd have a peaceful lunch mid-tramp.

Always, we were in it together, three loyal musketeers.

❖❖❖❖❖❖❖❖

Returning to this spot with our latest recruit, we had some good times the first couple of days. Devon took to the quiet hillsides, chased chipmunks, learned the country roads and paths. There was scarcely room in the cramped cabin for one more dog bed, but otherwise Devon seemed to fit right in. As a concession to his peculiar tastes, however, I found space in the vast local school playground where he could burn off some energy by tearing off after trucks, as usual, with a fence between them and him.

Then came the morning that I had to make a run to the

county dump. I left Devon outside with the Labs, who often sat keeping an eye on the mountain while I ran short errands. Knowing that everything with Devon became a chess match, and that he would without question cause trouble over this, I left the dogs, gave several elaborate "stay" commands complete with hand signals, and drove down the driveway.

Then I turned off the Trooper's ignition, crept out, and crawled up the slope that runs alongside the driveway. The scene was still for several minutes until, crawling right above me out of the bushes, moving slowly and silently, came Devon. My trap had worked.

I sprang out at him, throwing sticks, hollering, "No! Bad dog! Stay! Get back!" along with some choice curses. He tore back toward the house. I ran after him down the driveway, shouting. The Labs appeared, tails wagging, bewildered. Devon ran to the side of the house and cowered. "I know you, you little son of a bitch," I roared. "I told you to stay, and goddamnit, you'd better stay."

I tried this strategy twice more, turning the ignition off and waiting. No sign of the Helldog. When I drove back into the driveway, he was right where I'd left him. Progress.

Pleased, I drove the few miles to the dump. I wasn't gone for more than ten minutes, then headed home. My cabin sits at the top of a mountain, up a steep mile-long road bounded by meadows, houses, and woods. I had just turned up the road, when a sleek head peered furtively out behind the barn to my right. Devon. He'd waited until I'd sprung my silly traps, then hauled ass down the entire mountain in the direction my car had gone.

I slammed on the brakes and pulled over, jumping out of the car. He saw me and vanished. "Devon!" I roared. "Come here now!"

A flash of movement behind the barn. I glimpsed a blur of black and white moving up the mountain, disappearing quickly into the tall grass and trees.

I charged up the mountain as fast as the old Trooper could go in second gear, leaving clouds of dust behind me as I veered into the driveway leading to my cabin. I figured I'd have to walk all over the damned mountain to find him.

But Devon was sitting right out on the grass near the porch, between Julius and Stanley. All three tails were wagging. Only Devon was panting.

Next day, I felt secure about allowing the three of them to spend the pleasant morning outdoors. I often worked for hours without a break, and didn't want to keep the dogs cooped up the whole time, especially in spring sunshine. They could sleep, stroll around the meadow, meditate, or chase chipmunks as their distinctive natures dictated. Since I wasn't leaving, Devon would have no car to chase, no reason to run.

After ten minutes, I came out and checked on the trio. He was gone. Julius and Stanley looked a bit relieved. I yelled;

he didn't come. I patrolled along the driveway and the meadow; no sign of him. Getting that familiar, Devon-inspired, heart-thumping panic, I ran back and forth in the woods shouting his name. No answer.

I called the sheriff, the local animal warden, and the nearest vet to report him missing. Then I went out looking, driving up and down the mountain, yelling out the Trooper's window in a voice that was growing hoarse.

An hour later, panicky and frazzled, I returned to the cabin to wait by the phone for news that I feared might never come. A frightened dog could go a long way in this sparsely settled countryside without encountering a person or a house. He'd be traumatized. God, what an idiot I was. When was I going to get it?

I remember literally wringing my hands, I was so over-wrought. Devon had been through so much, come so far, only to be lost in the woods. By nightfall he'd be scared to death and completely alone. Wasn't this his worst fear? Why hadn't I teth-ered him or kept him inside? I kept calling the neighbors and making sweeps up and down the road. I was a wreck.

Two hours later, I went outside and called his name for the umpteenth time. I heard a rustle in the woods and out he ex-ploded, covered with burrs, bristles, and mud. He was as happy as I'd yet seen him, as overjoyed to find me again as I was to see him. His tail wagged furiously, and he kept leaping into the air to lick my face, whining and barking. I hugged him fiercely, too relieved to scold. He was relieved as well and rushed over to lick Julius and Stanley (who ignored him), then jumped back into my arms.

He didn't leave my side for the rest of the day. Sometimes you have to run off to figure out what home means. Having come all this way, it was clear to both of us that we didn't want to lose each other now. And though this wasn't the way I'd planned or hoped, we seemed to have bonded after all.

I believed at that moment that I could never send him back. It would destroy him and devastate me. I had to make this work. The alternative was hard work and patience. I had to find a way to do better.

Six

SHOWDOWN IN NEW JERSEY

"*Some border collies just don't really work out,*" said Ralph Fabbo, the ace trainer who had worked so successfully with Julius and Stanley. I was seeking his counsel, somewhat abashed because he'd cautioned me against having three dogs (Why mess up a good thing? he asked), and had pointed out that border collies can sometimes be too hyper and unstable to train for domestic life. He would undertake the job, he said, but it probably wasn't necessary. "You know what to do."

Did I? I called Deanne, too, to report on the troubles I was still having with Devon. Back home in New Jersey, he was attached to me, increasingly affectionate—but still jumping on tables, knocking things over.

One afternoon, he threw himself against one of the leaded-glass panels that framed the front door—perhaps our only elegant bit of household architecture—and shattered it with such force that the lead bent and contorted.

He showed little interest in his food, but sometimes he went after Stanley's or Julius's. He grabbed Stanley's bed, his rawhide chews, his favorite spot in the living room. It was especially troubling because Stanley wouldn't defend his turf. He didn't seem to have the heart to resist Devon's incursions. Nor did he have the energy. He seemed fatigued lately, lagging behind on our walks. Maybe just watching Devon was tiring him out.

In fact, walking the three of them together had become impossible. Dev turned around frequently while we walked to see where Jules was. At Devon's pace, we soon were strung out over a hundred yards, Devon lunging on the leash and pulling ahead, Julius sniffing behind us, Stanley panting even farther to the rear. This was dangerous: I couldn't really keep a careful eye on all three, and I worried about children racing by on bikes, or cars backing hurriedly out of driveways.

Our easygoing walks had become decidedly unpleasant, given my constant shouting at Devon to slow down or the Labs to hurry up. It was just the kind of life with dogs I didn't want to have.

My progress report to Deanne wasn't completely discouraging. Devon was coming to love Julius—though to be honest, there is no being, human or canine, who doesn't love Julius.

Despite his dark streak, Devon also had his good moods, especially when the morning was under way. Then he would trumpet a series of joyous *roo*'s, scaring the hell out of me and the Labs and charging off downstairs. It was the call to work; he was telling us to get off our asses and join him in the day's tasks, which he always undertook with great enthusiasm.

But our tasks weren't so simple. On the leash, Devon remained a nightmare, tugging and yanking. Off the leash, he was worse, galloping down driveways and into backyards, chasing across lawns after squirrels.

Deanne pondered my accounts. "He's like his mother," she mused. "Very headstrong and willful."

In fact, Devon was by far the most stubborn and dominant creature in the house, Paula said, with the exception of me.

Furthermore, having finally found someone he was beginning to attach himself to, he couldn't bear it when I left him; he was convinced I wouldn't come back. Or maybe he was just pissed off at being left behind.

Devon always wanted to come along—always. Beyond loneliness or neediness this was a display of the intense curiosity that characterized the breed. Border collies always wanted to be in on the action. Accompanying me on errands, he rode with his nose out the car window, then raced from one side to the other.

There was lots to see in New Jersey—cars, trucks, buses, other dogs, walkers, joggers, packs of kids—and he took it all in.

But when I left him in the car and went into a store, he jumped nervously between the front and back seats until I returned.

What occurred to me, with Deanne's help, was that Devon was finding me interesting, and had taken me on as his work. He was putting his pride, stubbornness, intelligence, and neediness into this new relationship. I had a strange, recurring feeling that Devon thought that with some effort, he could help me sort things out.

❖❖❖❖ ❖ ❖❖❖❖

"You can't keep a dog who's wild, who's behaving that way," Deanne warned. "You are either going to have to convince him that you can make him do what you want, and that you aren't going to abandon him, or he'll have to come back. Do you want to try?"

I understood this moment for what it was, a crisis between a dog and its overwhelmed new owner. I couldn't go on like this indefinitely. It wasn't fair to Devon, the Labs, Paula—or me. If I wasn't yet at the decision-making point, I was rapidly approaching it. Change is invigorating, but chaos is destructive. On the mountain, it seemed unthinkable to ship Devon back. Despite his running away, there were fewer issues or disputes up there. Back in New Jersey, life was a lot more complicated, and I felt less certain.

But there was no denying the mushrooming love I was feeling for this taxing creature, even in so short a time. If this conflict wore on much longer, I knew I really wouldn't have any choice; I wouldn't be able to send him away.

Deanne was giving me the out. She was telling me that this was the time to surrender and send him back. In my mind, I pictured the return trip to Newark Airport, where I would stuff him back into that crate and watch as the baggage handlers wheeled him off. Not an appealing image.

I was quiet for a moment. "I'd like to try everything possible," I said, "before I even think of giving him up."

Deanne was happy to hear it, but full of warnings. "It's going to be rough," she cautioned. "This is going to be a real test of wills, and the stronger one will prevail."

She and I were on the phone several times a week now, talking strategy, plotting techniques. Deanne was in medical school and could ill afford this distraction, but her devotion to her dogs was strong. Despite her workload, she was never impatient or reluctant to talk. She wanted this cross-species adoption to work.

"You are underestimating yourself," she advised. "You can do this."

Some of Devon's problems had probably come from his disappointing experience as an obedience dog, she thought. He seemed resistant, even sullen; he obeyed commands, but grudgingly. To subject him to a new person shouting commands could be counterproductive. So, no Ralph to tame the Helldog; the job fell to me.

"When Devon accepts you as the leader," Deanne said, "he'll roll over on his back and show you his belly. That's the gesture of submission. If he does that, you've won. If he doesn't . . ."

I went out and bought a shorter leash and two choke chains, one to put around his neck, one to toss and make noise with during training. I cleared my work schedule so I could concentrate on the looming confrontation.

I think Devon sensed that we were going to duke it out, and gave no quarter. In this context, we were both true to our natures. He could have given in, I could have looked the other way. Somehow, I didn't think that was going to happen. The battle was joined.

When it was time to go out walking, he lunged ahead of me and pushed open the door, sometimes breaking away to challenge people or other dogs outside. He jumped toward buses and trucks, sometimes pulling me down, or twisting my bad ankle. He got crankier about sitting, lying down, or staying, things he had actually begun to do.

The more insistent I got, the more he dug in. Deanne had nailed it: this was a battle of wills, and victory would go to the most stubborn and patient. I couldn't really say I had him beat on the first count, but I had an edge on the second.

As the campaign kicked in, I grew tougher with him, ordering him to sit, then throwing the choke chain at his feet if he didn't.

If he still wouldn't sit, I pressed my hand down on his rump until he complied. People in the neighborhood saw me chasing him through hedges and across lawns and wondered aloud why I hadn't been content with those two wonderful Labs. Devon seemed actually to grow angrier and more defiant as the training progressed. Perhaps this was a window into what had happened to him, why he'd been abandoned in the first place.

One time, he took my hand in his mouth when I pushed down on his hindquarters to make him sit. Openhanded, I swatted his rump so hard that my hand stung. Then I pushed down again, and he mouthed me again. I spanked him again. We repeated this three times before he sat, slowly and resentfully. I wasn't happy, either; I was growing too angry.

Other than a mild nose tap for a puppy, I'd never slugged any of my dogs. But I couldn't let him win this round. It would be the end of us, of his life with me and, perhaps, of his ability to live with anyone.

Exhausted, increasingly anxious, and frustrated, I was also increasingly resigned: I was getting nowhere. Perhaps my books were right: border collies weren't for everybody, and they weren't for me.

The morning after I'd hit Devon—who had neither flinched nor winced, nor seemed to really notice—I got up at 6:30 A.M., when I knew the streets would be quiet. It was a cool spring morning.

I gave Devon the "heel" command and he walked placidly alongside me for a few paces, then started creeping forward. This was the problem with Devon: even when he obeyed, he managed to subtly defy. His will was both impressive and infuriating. I praised him anyway, then leaned over to pet him.

As I did, he lurched, pulling the leash from my hand—for a medium-sized dog, he's extraordinarily strong—and charged into the street toward a small private school bus.

He leaped right in front of it. The driver slammed on his brakes, the tires screeched, and I heard a couple of kids yell in fright.

There was something shockingly willful about the incident. Devon was no dummy; he knew quite well that he wasn't permitted to run into the street—we'd been working on it ten times a day since he'd arrived.

I ran into the street, grabbed the leash, and, apologizing to the driver, roughly pulled him back onto the sidewalk. There I grabbed him by the scruff of the neck. "No! No! Bad dog!"

I sat down next to him on the curb and talked, more quietly but just as intensely, into his face. "Listen, pal, we're going to work this out or tomorrow only one of us is going to be here and it isn't going to be you. You understand me?" A neighbor on the way to the train to Manhattan had stopped in response to my yelling and gave me an odd glance. "Hey, you okay?" He was a great admirer of Julius and Stanley, who were back in the house, still dozing.

"I guess I'm not, not at the moment," I said wearily. In fact, I thought, I'm nuts for battling with this screwed-up dog.

Devon wore an expression of deep concentration. He was fearless about disapproval and physical punishment, though he did seem interested in an explanation. He was able to do anything I wanted, but really, why should he? Merely performing held no particular appeal. Was there a point?

How could I get through to him that this wasn't a silly command in an obedience event, that this meant the difference between his living with us, being my dog, and not?

We started off again, and he walked along perfectly and calmly. Once again, I reached over to pat and commend him—positive reinforcement—and, once again, he seemed to be waiting for an opportunity.

He lunged and was suddenly gone again, the leash slipping right through my chilled fingers, in pursuit of a bigger and louder school bus. This round, he threw himself at the moving front tire. It was especially horrifying. I thought he was within inches of being hit, but as the bus passed, he barked and jumped back.

There was something primal about the challenge Devon had

thrown down, even at the risk of his own life. This was pure, calculated defiance. I hadn't brought him to New Jersey to see him crushed under a bus. Simply put, I snapped.

I was not thinking rationally; I wasn't thinking at all. I wasn't recalling training manuals or border collie books or Deanne's good advice or my own instincts and experience. We were back in a prehistoric era, caveman and semidomesticated animal.

The bus rumbled away—the driver hadn't even seen him—and Devon stood tauntingly in the street, almost daring me to do something.

I was on him like a bear. I picked him up, one hand on his collar, the other on his haunches, and hurled him five or six feet onto the grassy strip next to the curb. He was light and agile and landed on his feet; he darted a few feet away, saw me charging, and stood his ground.

I have to give him credit: he would fire off like a rocket after a squirrel, or just for fun, but he would never duck a fight. He braced himself. He saw me coming and could have taken off in a flash. He didn't. And at that moment, I was beyond empathy. I threw the metal pooper-scooper at him, intending it to clang loudly on the sidewalk in front of him, but it skidded and hit him squarely in the shoulder, causing him to start. I threw the choke chain at him, too. I was screaming, cursing. This was no training technique, it was pure rage, a nearly unprecedented eruption from a veteran wuss.

I lurched onto the sidewalk, tripping over the curb and falling onto my knees. He was still standing there, watching me. I ran to him, smacking him in the side, knocking him into a shrub. "Don't you understand?" I shouted at him. "You can't stay here like this! You'll have to go back!"

I was panting and red-faced when a green Subaru station wagon pulled up alongside us, the window slowly rolling down. I turned and saw a woman and her daughter, perhaps ten, sitting beside her.

"Excuse me," said the woman in a particularly grating tone of voice. "But my daughter doesn't like the way you're treating your dog."

A classic and typical moment in my Boomer town. It might have been the whole scene, or it might have been that mommy turning even this into a child-welfare issue, but I was not inclined to have a discussion with this idiot.

"Lady, mind your own business!" I screamed. I was mortified—I couldn't recall ever yelling in public that way, let alone in front of a child. Ordinarily, I would have been only too happy to share my laments over this dog.

But. But. Doesn't like the way I'm treating my dog! Let her tour my fucking house and see the imported food, the multiple dog beds, the heaped collections of chewbones and balls and squeaky toys. Let her train this evil bastard! I was purple with fury.

I turned back toward Devon.

He was on his back, feet in the air, tail curled underneath, ears back so far they nearly folded into his head.

I stood frozen. We were both shaking; I'm not sure which one of us was more upset. Talking to Deanne earlier, I had made my decision. Now Devon had made his.

❖❖❖❖❖❖❖❖❖

The woman in the car may have been obnoxious, but she wasn't wrong. I don't believe in treating any dog the way I'd just treated Devon.

I can be moody and brooding, but I'm not a violent person. I've never struck another human being in anger, or spanked my daughter, or even, to my memory, shouted at her.

Apart from sparring with authority figures and editors who tell me what I can't write, I go to great lengths to avoid even minor confrontations. I can't bear to tell a cashier if I've been overcharged.

Yet I know there's plenty of anger in me. Devon rekindled some of that the minute he shot out of his crate, perhaps because he viewed the world the same way. And he'd been stoking it ever since.

I'd tried to keep that emotion in check. But that morning, I was terrified at the sight of his nearly being run over by a bus. And I was worn down, physically and emotionally, from the miles of walks, the constant shouting and correcting, the eternal vigilance required to prevent Devon from killing himself, driving the other dogs nuts, and wrecking our house.

I was also starting to resent his intrusion into my work. People who work at home, especially writers, are highly vulnerable to disruption; they need a lot of space and concentration, and mine was suffering. And I felt guilty about Julius and Stanley, who, for all their faithfulness, found themselves in the middle of a battle, their routines disrupted, our peaceful existence together made tense.

By this point, I thought taking Devon might have been a mistake. I was well aware that none of this was his fault. He hadn't asked to come. I knew he was just following his instincts, but it seemed that I was doing my part and he wasn't doing his. I thought our relationship wasn't going to work. At times, I couldn't bear this drama, which seemed to be pulling me back to dark places, where old feelings of fear and rage bubbled up. I knew what it felt like to be disliked, abandoned, and unsuccessful. We were soulmates, kindred spirits, on the same frequency to an amazing degree. But we were also driving each other berserk.

Had Devon been a person, and our relationship turned that confrontational, we would have gone into therapy together. There was no question that I had come to love him deeply.

Yet I had no trouble making the distinction. He was a dog. He had to accept my authority in ways I myself had furiously resisted my entire life.

If we could pull this off, we would make a great pair. We could make some bigger statement about both our lives, too: about patience, about rewriting history and healing wounds, about not giving up on each other, about not walking away. This was partly about faith and commitment. But that's a lot of baggage to put on a dog—too much.

❖❖❖❖❖❖❖❖

I understood instantly after the brawl that something of enormous importance had happened. Devon was transformed. At first, it was a wrenching sight, those flattened ears, the beseeching eyes. This was his Appomattox. He had fought long, hard, and with valor. He needed to be permitted to surrender with dignity.

I approached him slowly, knelt by his side, turned him over. He crawled into my lap, his head in my arms. The fear, confusion, and defiance seemed to peel away.

I felt for him. For a proud dog with centuries of independence in his blood to lie on his back in abject submission is a potent show of trust. Pressing his face next to mine, he licked me tentatively, once, twice, then a hundred times. His tail began to swish. I was no longer angry. In fact, I was deeply sorry. I had violated all my own principles.

"It's okay, boy," I told him. "I love you. You're home. You're home for good. I'll never abandon you, I promise."

I stroked his head and neck. "And I'll make a solemn promise to you. We'll go find some real sheep as soon as things settle down, and you'll get to herd them. I swear."

Devon's whole demeanor had changed. It was as though a different dog had emerged from the battlefield haze.

Some cars and more school buses came by. Devon didn't even give them a look, though we probably provided an odd sideshow for the commuters and schoolchildren, whose numbers were beginning to grow. A few of the drivers slowed for a closer look.

They saw, at the intersection in front of my house, a black-and-white dog, lying in the lap of a large man as if he'd been shot. Debris from the battle lay scattered around—the pooper-scooper, my baseball cap at the curb, his leash, a choke chain.

We both got to our feet and began walking down the sidewalk, chagrined and on our best behavior.

Some of the reasons for this change were obvious: Devon understood that he now had a leader, someone he had to obey. He knew his place in the pack. This seemed to calm him, soothe his anxiety. I think he understood my promise, which I could now make freely and could truly mean: now he could feel my love, relief, and appreciation. Whatever happened, this dog had a home with me.

I had gained his respect, or at least his obedience, in a primal way that felt utterly alien to me. But the brawl had allowed him to let go of something, old fears or struggles, resentment perhaps. We'd entered into a binding contract: he had decided to trust me. I had decided to love him.

Devon has let me know, since that morning, that he has by no means surrendered completely. Our conflict moved into a lower-intensity, guerrilla phase. Some of our struggles were, in fact, just beginning. But the war was over.

Since that brawl, however, he can walk off-leash almost everywhere, although I'm selective about where. He has never run away from me or darted into the street. He's never nipped at a child, chased a school bus, refused to come when I call. He has never jumped the fence or dug under it; he no longer tries to loosen the slats. He's damaged no more windows. He's lost all interest in leaving me.

Quite the opposite: he is eternally fascinated with me. I am his shepherd, his brother, his pal. He stares at me for long stretches and prefers, when possible, to keep me in sight. When I write in my study, he often sits in the backyard at the window that looks into my office.

We communicate with hand signals and the beginnings of words—I rarely need to finish sentences. He knows when we're walking, riding, when I'm taking him along or leaving him at home, when he has my permission to run, when he doesn't.

Inside, he sits at the doorway to whichever room I'm in, observing traffic and checking on my well-being. If I yell, cry, trip, grunt, shout, or make any unusual sound, he's at my feet in a nanosecond, looking me over, ready to serve, protect, defend.

He knows about my bad leg, and when I fall or stumble, which happens with some regularity, he's instantly at my side, worried, licking my hand, wanting to help. He's become Lassie-like. If I were down and in trouble, I'd have no hesitation about yelling, "Devon, boy, go on! Get help!" He'd zoom away and show up at somebody's door, barking frantically, leading them to where I lay. Maybe this is a fantasy. I suspect I'll find out one day.

I know him better now. Underneath all the hell-raising, he's a sweetheart, needy but also generous and giving, full of affection.

He is capable of great calm, a new addition to his repertoire. It was now clear that he'd known all along what I wanted from him, he just wasn't convinced he ought to do it. He stopped jumping on tables, knocking over phones, pacing in the house. He ate from his own bowl, left Stanley's alone, began to appreciate Julius and watch over him. Yet he retained his spirit and pride. He was still a working dog.

Old Hemp, smiling down from some moor in the sky, couldn't have been prouder. Or was it Old Kep?

Seven

LOTS AND LOTS AND LOTS OF HEART

Stanley was lagging, it turned out, because he was dying. It was hard to believe. His eyes still had their permanent playful gleam. He was the eternal sprite. Paula said Stanley was the cutest puppy that had ever lived, and he'd kept his sweet puppy face into his eighth year.

Dr. Brenda King is a great vet—direct, thorough, confident. She sometimes doesn't seem all that wild about people, but she's crazy about dogs and usually, after nodding briefly to their humans, speaks directly to them. Her diagnoses and instructions are brief and to the point, but they carry a lot of weight.

Stanley nuzzled her hello, then accompanied her willingly to the X-ray machine, throwing back an anxious look when he saw I wasn't coming along.

A little while later, Dr. King came in and closed the door behind her. Not a good sign. She knew my dogs very well, and was certainly aware of how close we were.

She had a particular soft spot for Labs in general, and for Jules, as she called him, in particular. She joked about his lack of enthusiasm for traditional Lab-like activities, and the resultant special diets we had to conjure up to keep him from ballooning like a manatee. And Stanley had always melted her heart.

"Bad news," she said in her usual, forget-the-b.s. style, but her eyes belied her professional mien. "Stanley's heart rate is way down, well below the last time we checked and far below what it ought to be."

She'd first noted a decline on our visit a few months ago, but at the time it was small and didn't appear to merit further attention. Now her examination revealed a different story. Besides which, she said, the X rays confirmed another suspicion—severe hip dysplasia, epidemic in Labs and golden retrievers. It was becoming painful for Stanley to run or walk too far; he was well on the way to becoming crippled. "I'm surprised he can even chase the ball," she said.

I thought silently that Stanley would happily chase a ball to his last breath.

But the steep decline in his heart rate was more alarming. I'd have to bring Stanley in a couple more times, once right after he got up in the morning, once after exercising. We'd run tests to make sure.

Devon wasn't in any way a factor, she was quick to assure me, anticipating the waves of guilt I was already feeling.

The news grew worse at each visit. Stanley's heart was failing. Apart from open-heart surgery, or powerful medications whose side effects could be dreadful, there were no good treatment options. And for me, those weren't options at all. I have a clear sense of how far I'm willing to go when a dog becomes seriously ill, what I'm willing to put a dog through, even one I care for as deeply as Stanley.

Dr. King didn't have to say what she was thinking. I'd been to see her dozens of times over the previous years. There was no encouragement or hope in her face or in her words.

❖❖❖ ❖ ❖❖❖ ❖ ❖

Even more than getting a dog, the biggest, most complex and wrenching decision in any dog owner's life is when to put a dog down. There are people who choose to keep their dogs alive by any means possible, just as there are people who choose that fate for themselves.

But I have to be honest: I am not one of them. The relationship between a dog and a human is always complicated. The two know each other in a way nobody else quite understands, a connection shrouded in personal history, temperament, experience, instinct, and love.

One's own life story is always inextricably bound up with

this decision, as mine was. Brenda King told me once that the great challenge in being a vet—or a dog owner—is a sense of advocacy. Unlike people, dogs can't speak for themselves. The lucky ones hook up with people who know them and fight for them, who act humanely and lovingly on their behalf.

People who grew up without advocates often get entangled with dogs, for the most obvious of reasons. Sometimes—any vet will tell you this—dog owners lose sight of the boundaries between their own lives and their dogs' lives, between the human and the canine experience. During any extended visit to a vet's office, ancient dogs in dreadful shape are carried or wheeled in for medications, operations, and devices.

"What you've got to do," Dr. King told me in her usual matter-of-fact way, "is to figure out not only what the dog wants, but what the best thing is for him. Nobody else can do that."

So I understood that my decision about Stanley wouldn't be born of the moment. It would be shaped by decades of personal experience, by the myriad factors that constructed my own worldview. And it would be a huge decision. I adored that dog, who unlocked the happy, playful parts of me. But I understood from the minute I left Dr. King's office what I was likely to do.

What would I want? What would Stanley want? What would be best for him? For him to end his life as happily as he'd lived it. For him not to be crippled by hip dysplasia, or felled by a stroke, heart attack, or seizure. For him not to end his days struggling to take a walk, chase a ball, keep up with the new pack that had abruptly formed in my house and life.

Several friends and neighbors pleaded with me to collect more opinions, consider surgery, try holistic healing, get on the Web, or explore radical new diets. One even suggested adoption: I could seek a quieter home, where Stanley could live peacefully and perhaps longer. I could visit him from time to time.

But sitting on the steps outside Dr. King's office, sniffling and hugging him, I felt as if I really would rather have died myself than give him away, break our extraordinary bond. I had to do the right thing by my lights, be true to my sense of his interests. I had to be his advocate and, of course, the advocate I always wanted to have and which I had come to understand finally I never would have.

I will never know, of course, if what I decided was the right thing. Nobody can say that with certainty. But I had a powerful sense of clarity, of knowing what I had to do for him. He needed that from me.

❖❖❖❖❖❖❖❖

Sweet Stanley. Every day began with his climbing into bed between Paula and me, curling up for an extended cuddle. I smiled every time I looked at his face. I couldn't help it. He continuously brightened my life with that happy spirit, that big heart.

He wasn't as mournful and contemplative as Julius, or as

smart or as weird as Devon. But he had more fun than any dog I knew. I'd had enormous joy watching his passionate, fervent ball-chasing and retrieving, on land and in water, to which he brought serious commitment and inexpressible pleasure.

He was my almost-oceangoing Lab—and his big heart, perhaps his most marked characteristic, was suddenly failing him. It seemed unjust.

But I wasn't surprised on that summer afternoon when Dr. King brought me the bad news for the third time, and Stanley came over and put his head between my knees, tail wagging. As always, he was concerned about me, sensing my unhappiness. I scratched his favorite spot, behind his ears.

Stanley was always toting something around the house. He loved retrieving the newspaper each morning, strutting proudly down the walk and into the house as if he'd bagged a pheasant, eagerly awaiting his biscuit and exclamations of praise.

In fact, there in Dr. King's examining room, he plucked a paper cup out of the waste can and began proudly walking back and forth with it, head up, tail wagging.

"I feel we should put him down," I said haltingly. "Does that make sense to you?"

She nodded. "When someone who loves his dogs as much as you do tells me that, it's time."

The alternatives were unacceptable to me. He'd tire and struggle, especially in the coming warm weather. He was at risk of seizures and heart attacks. I couldn't bear the prospect of his collapsing on a walk or during a swim. I feared he'd fade before my eyes.

I could see he had already lost much of his energy, and I felt especially bad about that. Once I thought about it, he'd been slowing down for months. Preoccupied with Devon, I hadn't been as quick to spot it as I otherwise would have. Dr. King was telling me it wouldn't have made any difference, but it made me miserable anyway.

Long walks were getting tough on Stanley, and though he still tore off after the ball, he might not be able to continue much longer. Too much swimming could be fatal, she said.

"Stanley has been happy every day of his life," I told Dr. King. "I'd like him to go out that way." I told her I'd need to talk to Paula, but I felt clear.

She agreed. She wished more of her clients' owners took that view, she said. One of the toughest parts of her work was keeping old and suffering dogs alive beyond their time, beyond reason. She mentioned a German shepherd who had no hind legs and was pulled around in a small wagon. She well understood the love of dogs, she said, but there came a point when there was little purpose or joy in a dog's life.

I didn't ever want Stanley to suffer that way. But I wanted to take him upstate to say goodbye. Up to me, Dr. King said.

I wanted to be careful, to make this decision on its own merits, without letting our three-dog drama subconsciously affect my judgment. The people who'd warned me about owning three dogs had been right—it *was* rough, the walks, the feeding, the attention each needed and deserved, the trips to the vet.

Our easy rhythms had been thrown off. Julius and Stanley were generous and forbearing, as always, but we'd had fewer of our special moments on walks or while I worked. Part of me missed having two easygoing dogs, and I didn't want that feeling to come near this decision. I asked Dr. King to backstop me, to tell me if there was any good reason to think that Stanley could get better, or enjoy more time. She said she would consider it carefully.

The tough part was, Stanley still took pleasure in life. He still loved Paula and me and Julius—though I don't think he loved Devon—and he would still happily chase balls, retrieve newspapers, and lick kids.

I wanted him to go out that way, before he got sick or knew pain or got scared.

We made a tentative appointment to euthanize him the following week. She asked if I wanted his body cremated, and I said yes. I pictured scattering his ashes upstate, in the woods and meadow and in the Battenkill, the place he most loved to swim and where both of us nearly drowned.

I drove upstate a few days later, with all three dogs. Devon was a different animal, but he was still a handful, and I wasn't sure Paula could handle him alone yet.

Upstate, the difference between this visit and the previous one was striking. Devon had become a Jon Katz scholar. He watched me all the time, closely enough to know that I was upset about something, and seemed to suspend part of his taunting rebellion and manic energy. He didn't stray once from the cabin.

❖❖❖❖❖❖❖❖❖

My plan was to give Stanley a perfect day, a proper farewell, and a hell of a good time. It was difficult, because several times, looking at him, I burst into tears and he tried to comfort me, which was completely backwards. I wanted to celebrate his life, not dwell with morbid anticipation on his death.

On his perfect day, I let the other two dogs outside and cooked Stanley a sirloin steak for lunch, feeding it to him in big, fragrant chunks. He couldn't believe his luck. I gave him three giant beef-basted biscuits for dessert. Then we went out onto the mountaintop.

Julius and Devon were lying beside each other staring out at the valley, a rare moment of calm for Devon, a premonition perhaps.

I threw Stanley's favorite mangled, blue, trapezoid-shaped ball, the one that bounced and jerked at crazy angles, and which he pursued with enormous enthusiasm, barks, pounces, and growls.

This ball had a history. It had been around nearly as long as Stanley had, and he'd treasured it from the first. It had probably been retrieved a million times, in all sorts of weather and on every conceivable terrain.

Once, he had chased it so intensely he plunged into a bush and got a sliver of wood stuck in his eye. I had to rush him to a nearby animal emergency center to have the splinter safely removed. As soon as he recovered, he went back to the bush and got his ball. Another time the ball got lost in a snowdrift in a park. A painstaking search by both dogs, our entire family, and several neighborhood volunteers failed to locate it. But as spring approached and the snow cover diminished, Stanley went back and dug it out.

One of his quirks was a fondness for leaning over storm sewers holding a ball and dropping it in with glee. I'd shout, but couldn't quite seem to convince him that this meant losing his beloved ball.

Whether he was being perverse or somehow driven by instinct, we lost many balls down many sewers. I tried to protect this favored blue ball—now pockmarked, misshapen, and disgusting—by not throwing it near sewer openings.

But one winter morning I forgot, and Stanley proudly walked to the edge of the sidewalk, leaned over the sewer entrance (one of my theories was that he was looking for raccoons and other creatures that lived therein), and dropped this ancient blue ball. It bounced on the grate and I tried to grab it as it ricocheted into the street, off the sewer entrance, back onto the sidewalk, and then—plop—down into the sewer. Stanley looked shocked, crestfallen.

Every day, every time we walked past that sewer, he would lean over, then turn and look at me beseechingly. But there was nothing I could do. To make the loss more painful, I couldn't buy him a replacement; the ball was no longer being manufactured. Stanley mourned.

But months later, during a fierce early-morning spring rainstorm, I was walking the boys and saw Stanley up ahead at the sewer entrance, barking and wagging ecstatically. I hurried over to the sewer and, to my amazement, saw the blue ball bobbing up and down in the murky water.

It had evidently been sitting down in the sewer well all these months. Days of heavy downpours had raised it close to street level, though it was still several feet down.

Stanley was overjoyed, looking at the ball, then at me. "It's in the *sewer,* Stanley," I said, pleading. "It's got to be disgusting. And it's freezing." But I knew. We all knew.

Egged on by his joyous yelps, I reached down with the pooper-scooper to try and snare the ball. The tool wasn't long enough, though, and the ball was bouncing crazily up and down, just out of reach.

Sighing and cursing, I lay down on the asphalt, protected only by my raincoat, and fished through the sewer grate with the scooper, water pouring over me. I didn't even want to think about what might be in the water.

Opening and closing the scooper to trap the ball, I came close several times, but whenever I thought I'd caught the damned thing, it would slip out. Stanley was intensely, expectantly focused on this rescue. Julius sat down in the rain and looked at me pityingly. I might be nuts, but he would sit it out with me.

I don't know how long I lay on that grate in the rain, but I suddenly became conscious of a car speeding in our direction, pulling up alongside me. I was also suddenly aware of flashing red lights. I lifted my head and saw a police cruiser and, coming up the street from the opposite direction, a unit of the town's volunteer ambulance corps. A door opened quickly and I was looking at a patrolman's boots.

"Hey there," said the officer.

"Morning," I said, my arms still extended into the sewer with the scooper. Was this illegal? I wondered.

At that moment, I got the ball! Julius came over to greet the officer—they were both friendly, I told him—but Stanley's eyes remained riveted on the ball.

"Mister, you okay?" asked the officer after a moment.

I couldn't let go of the ball now, after all this. I was trying the difficult maneuver of lifting it up and onto the street—it wasn't easy from this angle.

"Sure," I said. "I'm fine. Why wouldn't I be?" The ambulance had stopped a few yards away. "The dogs are friendly," I yelled as two paramedics hopped out and ran to me.

"Well, sir," the cop went on conversationally, "it's pouring, and it's six-thirty in the morning and you're lying on a sewer grate in the street."

I climbed to my knees triumphantly, with the scooper and—tada!—the ball. I kept the ball in the pooper-scooper, though. No way anybody was going to touch it until it had been boiled for half an hour.

"My dog lost his favorite ball," I explained meekly. The cop was speechless. I could only imagine how much he'd enjoy replaying this to the guys back at the station. For that matter, Paula would have a few choice words when she saw my clothes and coat.

One of the neighbors had looked out her window and seen me lying in the street, the paramedics reported. She'd naturally assumed I'd suffered a coronary and dialed 911.

What was there to say? I assured them that I was healthy, thanked everybody, and, mortified, turned to head for home.

"Wish I was your dog," the cop muttered, climbing back into his cruiser and driving away.

Fending off an overjoyed Stanley, I carried the ball home and boiled it.

But for Stanley's last visit, I'd brought it upstate with me and I threw it behind the cabin, a fraction of the normal distance. Stanley lunged happily after it, pouncing when he got close, then faithfully bringing it back to me. He took his retrieval duties very seriously.

A little later, we drove to Merck Forest, Stanley's favorite walking place. Something about the forest sparked him; he'd romp through the trees, woofing in delight, and bring me sticks and dead animal parts.

I left Jules and Devon in the Trooper, and Stanley and I walked down the trail a ways. I sat on a log and he came over and put his head in my lap. We had a long embrace. Then we visited his other haunts, the Battenkill and the lake, and I tossed the ball for him, stopping when he panted. I wanted to remember him healthy and vital and full of life.

Back at the cabin, we rested a while. I took him on as many walks as he wanted, fed him as many biscuits as he could eat, threw his ratty old ball again and again.

By late afternoon he was exhausted, and he curled up on his bed, breathing heavily, but still wagging his tail, licking me as I leaned over to hug him. He passed out until nearly nightfall.

Watching him sleep so peacefully, a part of me wished he

would die in that bed, and spare us both the next week, the waiting and dread.

A person who makes his living from words, I simply have none to describe what I felt. My friend Jeff said he couldn't look at me, there was so much sadness.

But I was overwhelmed with gratitude, too, for Stanley's companionship and love and cheerful presence during the past seven years.

At dusk, the other dogs and I accompanied Stanley on his last walk on the mountain, down the driveway, down the mountain road, into his favorite meadow, where he sniffed the flowers and weeds and stared up at the birds. I thought Julius and Devon seemed to hang back a bit as I walked alongside Stanley, but I might have imagined that.

The three of us had spent hours here, looking out at the magnificent views to the west, sharing lunch or a snack. I remembered the wind rising from the hills, sometimes gentle, sometimes brisk, caressing us, the Three Amigos.

When we got back, I offered Stanley the ball, but he didn't seem interested. It was as powerful a statement as there could be about what had to be done.

He passed up treats and biscuits, too, just lumbered over to his bed and didn't move again until the next morning.

But he had had an almost perfect Stanley day, and I felt good about that.

❖❖❖❖❖❖❖❖

Four days later, at eight A.M., I drove Stanley to Dr. King's office. Her receptionist asked if I wanted to be with him when he got the injection. Of course I did. I wouldn't let him die alone.

Dr. King barely said a word. "You sure this is the right thing?" I asked, and she nodded. We both knew the fewer words, the better. Besides, there was really nothing to say.

I sat on the floor with him, holding him, setting his blue ball down beside him. Dr. King injected a dose of yellow anesthesia into his rump. In a few minutes, he wouldn't be feeling anything, she said.

I felt an almost desperate panic. Maybe I should stop this; maybe it wasn't too late. But I fought back the urge.

"Thank you," I said, hugging him. "Thank you, thank you." He struggled to get to his feet, couldn't manage, looked bewildered and disoriented. He licked my hands, then started to cough and tremble. "I love you, pal, I love you, I love you." I couldn't stop crying now.

His eyes dilated and he lay flat on the floor, his legs splayed at an odd angle. I rearranged him so he would have more dignity, kept stroking him.

I wish there'd been a better, more pastoral place to do this, a sunny meadow rather than a cold linoleum floor. But Stanley probably didn't know where he was anymore.

A few minutes later, Dr. King came back into the room with another needle and asked if I was okay, if I was ready. I nodded. She injected the needle, and I put my hand on Stanley's big heart. I could feel it stop.

She listened with her stethoscope. "He's gone," she said.

I kissed him on his nose, patted his head, and left the room.

I knew there were lots of people in the waiting room, including kids, so outside the door I literally sucked it up, taking a deep breath. One of Dr. King's assistants wordlessly handed me some tissues. I said goodbye to the somber vet, who nodded and patted me on the shoulder.

The waiting room held the usual eclectic assortment of cats, dogs, and, over in one corner, a little girl clutching her rheumy-eyed puppy.

I smiled at her. "Don't worry," I told her as I left. "Dr. King will take good care of your puppy."

Eight

WEIRDVILLE

---

*S*oon after Devon arrived, I'd gotten an intriguing offer from the University of Minnesota: come this fall and teach a course of your own design about technology and culture.

The invitation stemmed from a column I'd written for Slashdot.org, the Web site that's my online home base, a geeky gathering place where I write a column about media, culture, and technology. The column in question was called "Mary Shelley, Frankenstein, and the Unabomber," and it discussed the bizarre way Americans create powerful new technologies but don't like to give much consideration to how they will be used. (Much the way, now that I think about it, we often acquire dogs.)

I liked Minneapolis and St. Paul and was keen on getting to know both cities better, and since Paula would be traveling to research a magazine story, it could be good timing. The U, as it is known, would let me come for a semester, or half of one, or just for a month.

The idea of spending a few weeks talking with students about the Net, the Web, and technology was a potent lure. Nobody knows this new world better than they do. My stint on campus might be good for them, but it would be great for me.

The offer came from Professor Kathleen Hansen of the communications department, whom I'd met earlier that year while on a book tour. The department's new media facilities were dazzling, and the students smart and down-to-earth. In addition, Kathy turned out to be the sort of person you can't easily say no to, and who pays scant attention if you do.

It was tempting, I told her. Usually I stayed clear of academe—the politics are too scary—but this could be a great way to teach: stay just long enough to meet people, learn something, and pass along a bit of what you know, then hightail away before it makes you crazy.

But I couldn't take her up on it. I had this new dog, I told her, a border collie, sort of a rescue dog, and if I left him alone with Paula for weeks, one of them might not survive. Besides, it would be awful for Devon if I took off at this point. He was just beginning to believe that I wouldn't.

Kathy didn't blink at this long-winded explanation of why I would turn down a nice gig at a prestigious university because of a high-maintenance dog. "Bring him along," she said. "We'll find an apartment that takes dogs, and maybe we can get you permission to bring him to class."

Hmmm. A cross-country trek with the Helldog would either cement our relationship or destroy it for good. It had a nice Steinbeckian *Travels with Charley* ring to it, Devon and me in a car for days.

"What if he were a therapy dog?" I asked.

"Is he?"

"Yes, he is." Technically true. I was amazed to learn from Deanne that although he was an obedience-show dropout, Devon had apparently also been trained as a therapy dog to work in hospitals with victims of strokes and other health problems.

I had actually taken him to the Kessler Rehabilitation Institute in East Orange to visit my dog-loving friend Pat—she'd had surgery, was recovering there, and had wangled permission to meet me and Devon in the lobby.

I was skeptical—this was a place where the Helldog could wreak serious havoc—but because Pat pleaded, I drove over, put him on a leash, walked across the parking lot and into the lobby. Here the ever intriguing Devon metamorphosed again.

Three people were sitting there in wheelchairs, and all of them nearly wept, they missed their own pets so much and wanted so badly to visit with Devon. Warily, holding him on a short leash, I walked him over to where the patients—two were amputees—were sitting.

Devon walked up to the first chair and dropped to the ground. The elderly woman reached down to stroke him, and he licked her hand gently, his tail swishing.

Then he walked to the second wheelchair and repeated the behavior—dropping to the ground, never jumping up or pawing, allowing himself to be petted, giving his cooing admirers a lick or two, then moving on. When Pat was wheeled off the elevator, he came over and did the same thing.

He *was* a therapy dog! Think of all the grief I could have saved myself if I'd bought myself a wheelchair to ride around the neighborhood in. We visited Pat daily, and Devon was such a gentle, well-behaved smash that the nurses all assumed he was duly certified (Deanne says he is, though I've yet to see any documentation) and invited me to visit a couple of wards. We did.

He proceeded with astonishing quiet, sensitive to whomever he was visiting. If someone couldn't manage to reach down, he'd put his head in his or her lap for stroking. It seemed his bad behavior was reserved for people who told him what to do.

This ushered in a whole new phase in our relationship. I began bringing Devon everywhere—to the dentist, the bookstore, a lecture at Princeton. It helped that in contemporary America, practically the worst crime is being insensitive. I walked Devon into the local CVS and was stopped by a security guard.

"You can't bring a dog in here, pal."

"He's a therapy dog."

"Oh, sorry. Sorry. Please forgive me."

I used this almost honest tactic everywhere, to Devon's great joy, since he loved going places with me—any place—entering new realms and receiving *ooh*'s and *aaah*'s from throngs. At the pet store, at Starbucks, no one ever asked me for proof of his therapeutic status, or even inquired as to what my particular need for a certified therapy dog might be.

In truth, the one for whom this practice proved therapeutic was Devon. With each visit, his confidence and social skills grew. He loved coming along, seeing new sights, and meeting the public. He seemed to realize for the first time that he was a gorgeous dog, and that people were eager to pet him and talk to him. Eventually, he became puzzled if somebody didn't.

I could almost hear him working it out: "No sheep around here, but this isn't so bad. I get to go every place and people actually like me. They really, really like me!"

And what institution in all of America is the most sensitive and socially conscious of all? By far, academe.

Two days after we'd talked, Kathy Hansen called back. "I told the administration you had to bring a therapy dog to class, and they said fine," she said. I'm sure she sniffed a scam, but she didn't really care. She was determined to get me out to the U.

I did eventually get one call from a university administrator, who, with many apologies and much sensitivity, asked me—she had a form to fill out—exactly what the nature of Devon's "therapy" was.

Oh, it's simple, I said. I have a bum leg (true) and fall down a lot (true). Devon's job was to steer me away from holes and rough pavement. "Thank you," she said. "I am so sorry for having to ask."

My initial plan was that Julius and Stanley would remain at home with Paula. They had often stayed behind when I traveled to research magazine pieces or books, enjoying their time in the backyard. A month would pass quickly. They'd keep each other company and give Paula no trouble. And then, soon after I'd agreed to spend October in Minnesota, there was only Jules.

Jules was the opposite of Devon—patient, secure, very attached to Paula, and generally content with his lot in life. He didn't like long-distance drives or disruptions of his routine. As for his state of mind, he seemed somber when I came home from the vet without Stanley, somewhat mopey and low-affect for much of the summer. But then, Julius was never particularly demonstrative. I have no doubt he missed his friend, but he rarely showed it in ways I could measure.

So, after some agonizing about leaving him—though he'd been without me before, he hadn't been without Stanley in years—we agreed. The adventurous Devon and I would head west. Jules would stay where things were comfortably familiar.

We made elaborate arrangements for Marilyn Leary—the professional dog walker he loved—and various dog-owning friends in the neighborhood to come visit and to help Paula walk him frequently.

Once all that was arranged, I wasn't worried about him. Julius was a very grounded dog, eternally good-natured. Though I would dearly miss his sweet gaze and companionship, he'd be fine. As for Paula, she accepted short absences from me with disturbing enthusiasm.

The next crisis, I told Kathy, was that I didn't want to crate Devon and put him on a plane. I'd seen how well that worked. No problem, she said; the school would rent a car.

The only problem was that almost no apartment building in Minneapolis or St. Paul, it turned out, offered short-term leases for people with pets. In fact, the U had found only one—a vast garden-apartment complex for in-transit corporate execs, military personnel, and other new arrivals in a northwest suburb called Plymouth. It lacked charm, apparently, but I figured we'd survive.

In late September, Devon and I drove west on I-80 in a small rented Oldsmobile, bound for Minnesota.

Surprisingly, we had a fairly pleasant trip. I put a dog bed on the backseat, and Devon settled there for long periods. I kept the windows closed, unwilling to risk any lunging incidents, but now and then he put his head on my right shoulder and gazed at the onrushing highway, as vigilant and conscientious as any captain on the quarterdeck in a Patrick O'Brian novel.

He rode that way for hours, taking a break to bark at trucks passing in the opposite lanes, taking in the view, too—the Pennsylvania woods, the Ohio factories, the Indiana traffic.

At rest stops, we relieved ourselves and refueled, and we also found a way to provide Devon the exercise he needed. The stops were off the highway, often bordered by long narrow strips of grass.

By now, Devon never chased anything without a special signal from me—a hand wave and the words "Go get 'em, boy." He'd bark and shoot off, galloping about a hundred yards or until the grass ran out, then turn on a dime and roar back even faster, Hemp-like.

He'd even locate the proper spot. At rest stops, he'd hop out of the car, trot over to a long grassy stretch, turn and stare at me. If I said no, we'd keep looking. If I said yes, and sounded excited, he'd drop into the classic herding position: head and tail down, eyes focused on the horizon, crouched and ready to spring on command.

Big, rumbling trucks remained his favorite quarry. He could hear their special sound before I even spotted them and would go into the crouch. I'd hold my hand out in the "stay" position—he scrupulously observed this—until a truck drew almost even with us. Then I'd wave my hand and shout, "Go get 'em," or "Okay!"

He'd explode like a shell from a cannon, his legs pumping so fast they were a blur, running as far as he could, then turning. We often drew an admiring crowd after two or three trucks. But he hardly acknowledged the praise; when he was working, Devon was undistractible. He loved this "work" even more in the rain, when the truck tires hissed on the road.

As it turned out, he also loved McDonald's cuisine. After some intense truck-herding, I'd tie his leash to an outdoor picnic table in sight of the restaurant, go inside, and order him a Quarter Pounder with Cheese and fries. I'd get a chicken sandwich, or hold out for something lighter elsewhere. He was also wild about Egg McMuffins in the morning. Back outside, we'd chow down and I'd pour him some cold water. Then, back on the road.

He couldn't have had more fun if he'd been in northernmost Wales, tearing through the ravines after errant livestock.

The first night, I pulled over at a Howard Johnson's in Cleveland, Ohio. Even this was Devon Heaven.

The motel sat on a bluff right above I-80, a giant chain-link fence separating a long strip of weedy lawn from the road below. Half the trucks in the world seemed to be rumbling right below us in the darkness. You could hear them and see their headlights miles away.

It was a cool but not uncomfortable night. I was too tired from driving to read or go out. I had a lot more driving ahead. But this was perfect recreation: Devon and I had a blast sitting on that bluff. I became adept at spotting the biggest, loudest tractor trailers, and Devon, at my signal, took off down the strip in hot pursuit, coming back to do it again.

After an hour or so, we reluctantly walked back to our motel room and I called Paula. "We had a great evening," I reported. "We were out chasing trucks on I-80. We're both exhausted and ready for bed."

There was a longish pause. "Sounds great," she said. "Travel is broadening."

After that, we picked motels carefully, keeping the truck-to-fence-to-grassy-strip ratio very much in mind. Devon got the motel routine down quickly. He'd wait until I was asleep, then hop into bed. I generally awoke with his head on one of my shoulders. He was a happy, calm creature. I was grateful, every time I looked at him, that he had come into my life.

We munched and herded ourselves halfway across America, Devon's head on my shoulder, helping me to navigate, for nearly two thousand miles.

❖❖❖❖❖❖❖❖

I instantly nicknamed the apartment complex where we were staying "Weirdville."

It was twenty-five miles outside Minneapolis, a tiring commute and a big sacrifice to have made for any dog, even Devon. I wouldn't be able to explore Minneapolis or St. Paul as much as I'd wanted, but this was the only place that would take dogs, even therapy dogs.

It was a monument to the new global economy, a sort of way station for disconnected Americans in transit—government employees being transferred, executives moving, people whose real estate purchases had fallen through, all sorts of folks between homes for one reason or another.

Nobody meant to be here; nobody planned to stay long. People arrived and vanished regularly, overnight; there was no point in making friends, as everyone seemed either shell-shocked or about to decamp.

The only other thing we all had in common was dogs. The complex stretched for miles and there were dogs everywhere, dozing on balconies, barking through apartment doors, being walked on the grounds and around the nearby lake, running free on tiny patches of grass.

The scene was as bizarre as it was hilarious. Dogs would pop out of every door—some leashed, some not. They would occasionally leap off the second-floor balconies. Many of them were big dogs, obviously not used to apartment living. They spent much of their time barking at the other dogs.

The best news for us was the lake, where Devon could run off-leash on the surrounding trails and walks.

Even better, we found—actually, Devon found—a long stretch of fenced park next to a highway streaming with trucks at all hours. I let Devon race back and forth till he dropped.

His capacity to adapt to completely new routines was impressive. In the morning, after his run, we'd drive into Minneapolis and park in a garage near the U. For the first week, he freaked in the garage elevator, then he got used to it.

Across the street, three blocks from the building where I taught, a funky café sold coffee, bagels, and sandwiches. Throngs of kids passed by on their way to class.

I'd tie Dev to a utility pole and go inside and order breakfast to go, while outside lines of people formed to pat Devon and exchange hugs and kisses. He loved the attention. I'd see him looking through the café window at me. *Is this okay?* he seemed to be asking. *Can we have this much fun?*

Whatever had been ailing him when he arrived in Newark that spring, Minnesota went a long way toward healing. Border collies are more common in the Midwest; many students at the U come from farming regions and know border collies. Some students would get nostalgic for their own dogs, dogs of sainted memory or merely dogs they'd left at home and missed. They'd reach into their backpacks and give Devon bits of sandwiches.

Eventually, the café owner noticed Devon tied up in the rain one morning and chastised me—for not bringing him inside. He became the place's mascot, going from table to table to greet patrons. He had a gift for knowing when he wasn't welcome. He'd go to a table, sit, and wait. If nobody responded, he'd simply move on. If someone seemed interested, he'd offer a paw and accept a gift. He never had to go far. Armed with takeout coffee, we'd next walk to Murphy Hall.

There are times when institutional sensitivity can really make a difference. Devon and I owe the U a lot. The students and professors couldn't have been more generous. They were perfectly entitled to give me a hard time, but no one did. In fact, Dev had legions of fans.

Inside, he went to see his particular friends Jon and Karen, sitting outside their offices. If they were in, they'd call him and ply him with dog biscuits. Half a dozen people volunteered to take him on walks while I was busy or in class. This strange creature, who just a couple of months earlier would have jumped out a window if I left him, became the BDOC. He seemed to especially love women. After a slight hesitation and a look back, he'd go off happily with his new walkers. Reports streamed in of his affability, good nature, and growing fascination with the slow, overfed campus squirrels.

In class, once I started talking, he'd sink to the floor and go to sleep. Two or three kids began bringing biscuits here, too, so that my opening comments were generally accompanied by steady crunching.

After the first few days, I could say, "Let's go to class," and he'd bound down the stairwell to the classroom. When I said, "Let's go to the office," he'd scamper back up.

At a colloquium for several hundred students and faculty in a big auditorium, Devon and I both took the stage. He sniffed until I began my talk, then settled down for a two-hour nap. He awoke to a polite round of applause, assuming, I'm sure, that it was for him.

At lunchtime, the two of us walked the banks of the Mississippi, where he'd run through the parks and along the walkways that bound the river.

Then it was back to my office, where I researched and wrote, and he'd curl up in a corner on the dog bed I'd brought along.

He couldn't believe his good fortune. He was with me every minute of every day, had tons of things to see and observe, and had crowds of admirers.

Back in Weirdville, he'd sit out on the patio and catch the cool evening breeze, monitoring and occasionally barking at the assortment of other dogs sitting on patios—poodles, shepherds, pointers, mutts, little yippy terriers—all woofing and whining in a strange, alienated chorus.

I did leave him alone at times—if I went to the movies, to dinner with students or professors, or to the local laundry or supermarket. But during that whole month, I doubt we were apart for more than twenty or thirty hours.

I missed Paula and Julius more than I'd expected, and I loved the kids and the class more than I thought I would. But the effects of the trek to Minnesota with Devon were the most surprising development of all. We bonded on that journey, as he kept a sometimes lonely, disoriented middle-aged man excellent company.

We took good care of each other. We learned to trust each other. Devon taught me something about patience and fidelity; he got a home and friend for life in return.

We had a sweet month in Minneapolis, for all sorts of reasons. Not the least is that I found some of my lost faith there in Weirdville, with a border collie who knew what it was to be lost, and then found.

Nine

HOMER

---

*B*ack home, Paula reported that Julius seemed subdued—more subdued than usual, which was already pretty subdued. But he was sunning himself in the yard, as usual, receiving his many human and canine pals, perhaps enjoying the fall colors. She said he seemed fine.

Even from Minnesota, I kept up my weekly yaks with Deanne, who loved hearing reports about Devon's progress and his embrace of academic life. It was fun to talk with her. She saw life with border collies as an intellectual challenge, and by now I could only agree.

We continued to trade strategies on overcoming his past problems, inducing his cooperation. She didn't like my practice of letting him chase after cars and trucks, even from behind a fence, although she understood that it had become a channel for his energy and part of our routine. But even before she challenged the practice, I knew I'd have to find some substitutes; it was ultimately too risky a game. One day he might misinterpret a command or forget himself—too many border collie owners told such stories.

As it happened, a new diversion soon emerged: the Canadian geese who also inhabited Weirdville began to attract Devon's fascination.

Geese out in the far Midwest are fat and cheeky. Many no longer bother to fly south for the winter, since there's so much tasty garbage left about by humans. Minneapolis is a beautiful city, but it isn't enhanced by the goose excrement that carpets much of its green space, especially along its famous lakes.

During my second week walking Devon through the park nearby, several parents came up to me one afternoon, kids in tow, to ask if he was a border collie. It was the first time anyone in Weirdville had actually spoken to me, and I figured they were about to ask me to put him on a leash when we walked, which they would be perfectly justified, legally and otherwise, in doing.

But that wasn't it.

They had heard about border collies, the parents said tentatively. And they wondered, well, here was the problem: their kids couldn't play soccer on the fields near the complex without stepping in and slipping on smelly goose droppings. Sometimes the geese took over the field and could not be scared off and the kids couldn't play at all. Was there any chance of my walking Devon out there, letting him have a run at the geese?

He seemed to puff up at the mere request, the genes of Hemp and Kep perhaps stirring a bit.

Sure, I said. Why not try it tomorrow morning, a Saturday? I was as curious as they to see if Devon's instincts might serve some actual purpose besides driving me nuts.

This would be a good chance to channel his instincts in a different direction. We had plenty of unwelcome goose shit in New Jersey, too, even if the geese didn't look as big or bellicose as these.

I'd heard lots of stories about how tough geese could be, how they'd stand their ground against people and dogs. Julius and Stanley had adopted the same attitudes toward geese that they had for most wildlife—they seemed not to notice them, always managing to gaze in some other direction.

How would Devon respond? After this parental SOS, I'd gone online to a favorite border collie Web site and posted a query about goose-herding. Border collies, it turned out, were often bought or rented for use at parks, corporate campuses, playgrounds, and country clubs to handle this very problem. "Just bring him there, and tell him to stay," one owner advised me. "Make sure he doesn't run until you give the command. He'll see the birds moving and figure it out."

Next morning we strode importantly to the field. Some of the parents who'd approached us stood by the fence, along with other soccer parents, a few coaches, and players.

In front of us, about fifty yards away, maybe two hundred sizable, swaggering, honking geese thronged the field. If they noticed Devon or me, they gave no sign of it, and they certainly showed no inclination to move.

Devon was a bit puzzled, looking at me, then at the fence where he usually chased after trucks on the other side. He paid no mind to the growing crowd, until a few of the kids started to cheer him on, "Go, Devon! Go, Devon!" That caught his attention. He dropped into what I called his "launch" position—eyes wide, head almost to the ground, ready to spring.

I cranked him, too, making my voice excited. "You ready? You ready? You ready?" I said it louder and more enthusiastically each time, laughing at myself. Another bizarre man-and-dog scene, halfway across the country on a huge suburban soccer field. "Maybe we should call the Discovery Channel," I yelled to one of the coaches.

He wasn't in an ironic frame of mind. He wanted his team to play. "Yeah! Go, Devon!" he yelled back.

Devon was fully amped by now, tense, alert, looking at me, then ahead. The geese began honking and Devon seemed to focus on them for the first time. I had a bright idea: we walked to the left and circled the field, putting the highway and its tempting trucks behind us, the geese front and center.

More parents and kids had arrived. This was becoming a matter of pride.

"Old Hemp is watching you, pal," I whispered to Devon. "Don't screw up." He cocked his head; I was asking something of him, but he wasn't sure what. That made two of us.

But when a group of geese began moving, he started to get it. Besides, he needed to chase something now or he'd bust. He went more deeply into his crouch.

"Good boy," I said, standing in front of him. His eyes were darting from my upraised hand to the geese, never taking his focus off either for more than a fraction of a second. "Are you ready? Ready, boy?"

Finally, I waved my hand, and yelled, "Devon, GO GET 'EM!" He sprang off down the field before the words had left my mouth, kicking up puffs of dust as he went. The geese turned to face him as he circled the flock, crouching down low, checking things out. Two of the birds, true to their reputation, stepped forward, prepared to do battle.

Good luck to you poor bastards, I said to myself, a battle-scarred veteran of many confrontations with Devon. I could see he was getting ticked off at their nonchalance. He began barking furiously, charging, nipping, darting behind the two leaders to cut them off from their reinforcements, then turning and lunging at the others.

The ghost of Old Hemp was definitely hovering above that soccer field. Devon's ancestral honor was on the line.

Suddenly, he circled back toward me, then turned and rushed at the ringleaders, and they began to have second thoughts about this black-and-white missile hurtling at them. They took to the air. Devon wheeled and charged behind the rest of the flock, barking and snapping furiously.

There was a great whoosh, a flapping and honking as the herd lifted off, complaining, and a cheer went up from the crowd. "Yeah, Devon! Attaboy, Devon!"

Devon tossed off a final contemptuous bark, and rushed happily back to me, tail wagging, ears up, chest out—one very happy dog, come to receive his plaudits. I told him, fishing biscuits out of my pockets, how canny and courageous he had been, a credit to his breed.

Some kids came running up to us, and I reached for the leash and tried to wave them off. But Devon wasn't about to spoil his triumphant moment. His tail wagging like the pendulum of a grandfather clock, he was receiving pats, hugs, handshakes, kudos, and kisses and acknowledging them with nuzzles and licks.

We went home and I did some work, then returned after the game. The geese came back four or five times—I couldn't tell if it was the same crew or fresh contenders—but Devon needed no further encouragement. At the field, he'd go into his crouch. By the third round, he could clear the field in sixty seconds. This was as swell as chasing trucks, though he occasionally gave the highway a wistful glance.

One time, a town police cruiser pulled over to watch the show; a parks department truck came by to tell me we were welcome anytime. So we made twice-daily visits to the soccer field, more on weekends. Devon's fans increased as the goose droppings diminished. When we left, they missed us in Weirdville.

I called Paula to relay the triumph. We talked about recouping the costs of rawhide and vet care by renting Dev out to golf courses in New Jersey.

What I didn't tell her was that I'd had a particularly interesting conversation with Deanne. Her new twelve-week-old litter included, she said, one of the sweetest, most loving puppies she'd ever had. But he had a mild case of something called "collie eye anomaly," a genetic defect that strikes the breed with varying degrees of seriousness. It wouldn't necessarily affect his vision, but it meant that he couldn't be bred or shown, so she was seeking a home for him.

And while I had my hands full, she couldn't help thinking what a perfect companion this dog would make for Devon. This pup had no unhappy history or emotional problems, had a pliant, submissive personality. He'd be a playmate, but never challenge Devon's authority or position.

But she'd have no problem finding a home for this puppy, Deanne added. In fact, he was so lovable she was considering keeping him herself. "Sometimes," she wrote me in an e-mail, "you get one that you just can't let go of."

She sent a digital photo along, just so I could see him.

◆◆◆◆◆◆◆◆◆

A diabolical move. She knew what would happen the instant I glimpsed the photo of that fuzzy, bright-eyed face.

Of course, another dog was folly. I had just learned that three dogs was one too many. Still, a name popped into my head: Homer. He was Homer.

"I can't really take on a puppy right now," I e-mailed back, and she said of course not. Hadn't I just been through a hand-wringing ordeal? She was just thinking aloud.

Merely out of curiosity, I asked how a young dog would affect Julius and Devon, who was finally feeling secure. Well, she was sure Julius wouldn't mind. He would likely be relieved to feel less pressure to play. (Probably true. Devon would often rush past with a toy, urging Jules to run with him. Julius would sigh, look at me, and sit down somewhere else. He might, in fact, be delighted to watch two lunatic border collies chase each other around.)

Besides, Deanne added, Julius was totally secure in his relationship with me. If he hadn't been threatened by Devon, he certainly wouldn't be threatened by this docile little puppy.

She pictured it this way: Homer and Devon out romping in the yard or upstate, chasing things, digging holes, wearing each other out, Jules dozing in the sun or stretched out by my feet while I worked, as usual.

Actually, she pointed out, that configuration would in some ways be easier. The two collies would exercise each other, so I could walk them less. And Devon would train Homer in a snap. But this was just friendly chatter, she added hastily.

I had plenty of dogs. She was messing with my head. Although . . . she was perceptive; she knew me and Devon; and if she said this pup was one of the most special she'd ever bred, then he was. Deanne was honest, blunt, and to the point. And there was some logic to her pitch (which, of course, was what this elaborately casual musing was). I was trying to wear Devon out, but more often, it worked the other way around. Maybe Jules and I could be a pair, and Homer and Devon could be a pair. It might make some sense, apart from the work of training, the clouds of dog hair, the vet bills, the walking . . .

I was doomed. I e-mailed Deanne back. "No fair," I protested. "That dog is totally adorable. How can you do this to me again? Think of Devon and Julius."

She wrote back: "I think Devon would have some adjusting

to do, but then again, he already shares some of your attention with Julius, and he did with Stanley while he was there. . . . Sharing is not always a bad thing :). I think you can offer more than enough love and attention for two borders, and I do think they will become each other's best buddies—even if they might be known to be a bit jealous of who is getting your attention at the moment, now and then. . . .

"Homer's just so cute (and not just his looks, he's got a bright, sweet heart as well). I don't want you to take him if you're not ready . . . seriously. There will be other nice pups in the future. But this is one of the pups we have every once in a while that stands out . . . so if you are ready, I think he'd be fantastic for you."

I was mulling it over all the way home from Minneapolis, but I made no commitment. Then, three weeks after I'd returned, I flew to Chicago to appear on the *Oprah Winfrey Show* in connection with my earlier book, *Running to the Mountain*. Oprah's producer had flown upstate with a crew to shoot footage of me and Paula, Devon and Julius the week before. The camera rolled as we walked along the lake and across the meadow.

During the show, Winfrey, whose warmth surprised me, watched the videotape closely. At a commercial break, she leaned forward, close to me. "Those are beautiful dogs," she said, in the recognizable tone of a dog lover. "I have a bunch myself. Is that a border collie?"

I briefly filled her in on Devon's saga. It was easy to see why Winfrey was so successful: she was one of those people you just want to sit and yak with. I wasted no time in seeking her counsel.

"Ms. Winfrey," I confessed to the high priestess of TV, "the breeder has a border collie puppy she says is sweet and loving. I'm agonizing about taking him."

She leaned closer, interested, meeting my gaze. This was not a face one could lie to.

"Do you want the dog?"

"Well . . . yes. I don't know why, but I do. Very much."

"Then take him, Jon," she said, more a command than a suggestion. "Make yourself happy."

She leaned back, the camera lights came on again, and we finished the interview.

I rushed to my cell phone after the show to call Paula, who probably thought she had heard it all. She knew about the puppy, of course, and had gone immediately to a DEFCON level-one alert, but I'd assured her this was mere fantasizing. She, of course, knew better. Now this.

"Honey, great news," I said. "Oprah says we should get the puppy!"

"What?"

"Oprah! Oprah Winfrey just told me to take Homer if it will make me happy. And it will."

"Oh, God," was all she said.

Ten

COMING AND GOING

Remembering my previous initiation rites, I asked Deanne to ship Homer to Albany—an even longer flight than Texas to Newark, but a quieter, less frantic airport. We'd have a calmer introduction. And going to the mountain after I picked him up would be a better way for all of us to get to know one another.

This was going to be fine. Homer was happy and fun-loving, Deanne reported; he hadn't known a nasty moment in his six-month life. He wouldn't challenge Devon or usurp him. Devon could be king, prince, leader, and big brother. Homer didn't care about canine politics. "This is one of the few dogs Devon won't ever feel threatened by," Deanne promised.

I had few worries about Julius, who enjoyed his morning walk, but slept pretty much the rest of the day. He was probably blue without Stanley—he had to be—but he was also slowing down, very content to be around me and Paula. No problems there.

As for me, this latest adoption surely had some connection to losing Stanley, but I was too busy writing and dog-walking to figure it out. So on a November night I found myself driving to Albany Airport, an hour or so from my cabin. I left Devon in the Trooper's backseat while I went in to meet the new guy.

This time, as the plastic crate was rolled out into the baggage area, I heard cooing from the two baggage handlers, both of them women. "He's so sweet," one of them said. "He's been trying to lick us. What a doll!"

I opened the crate—just a crack!—and eased my hand in. Homer edged toward the back. Something about me had frightened him; he was shaking. I reached, slipped the leash onto his collar, and gently pulled him from the crate. Confronted by a large stranger in a Yankees cap, the bright lights, and the airport carousel, he looked terrified. I picked him up, and a Good Samaritan watching our hesitant drama offered to carry the crate.

The thing about Homer that struck me then, as it does now, was his eyes—bright, curious, a bit mischievous. He was much smaller, thinner, more awkward, and less imposing than Devon, with puppy fuzz instead of a glossy, dark coat. If Devon looked a little like a wolf, Homer suggested a small fox. Devon had all the carriage and beauty of a show dog. Homer was built to run and play. He was cute, which Devon was not.

Like Devon, though, he took in every sight and sound, his head tilting to the side if he heard something odd or intriguing.

Outside, I thanked my benefactor and led the quaking Homer around so that he could meet Devon. What a sane contrast to Devon's arrival.

Off-leash, Devon was usually indifferent to dogs. Some breeds—shepherds and golden retrievers especially—trigger his herding impulses, but he loses interest once he realizes that they aren't livestock. He's never bitten or attacked a dog, though he's nipped at a few who get too enthusiastically in his face.

So I was stunned when I opened the Trooper's door and Devon came snarling out and instantly had Homer on the ground as he went for his throat. Homer shrieked.

I kicked Devon away and he looked at me in outrage. His attack couldn't have been more clear: I know what you're up to, he was saying, and there is no way this runt is coming into our car, our house, our lives. I've earned my place, and there's no room in it for *him*.

Homer—who, I later realized, had a strong sense of the dramatic—was squealing as if he were being murdered. I picked him up and put him on a blanket on the front seat, reaching back and cuffing Devon on the shoulder for good measure. Devon gave a couple of throaty growls, which caused Homer to scream again. I turned to the back, placed one hand firmly on each side of his face, and hissed that this dog was coming to live with us and if I heard another growl I'd mash him into the seat. Devon gave me a murderous look, got the message, but was unrepentant. Homer curled up in a ball and nibbled gratefully on the tiny biscuits I'd brought him while I stroked his head.

He was still a baby, a fluffball in a brown-gray shade that breeders call "blue." His ears stood at attention. And he largely ignored the fact that Devon was watching him like a hawk zeroing in on prey. All during the drive home, Devon glowered angrily over at me from the backseat.

I stopped in the village at my friends Jeff and Michelle's house because their two-and-a-half-year-old twins wanted to see the new puppy. I watched carefully. When I brought Devon over for the first time, he had run off Jeff's good-natured mutt, Lulu, and had nipped at one of the kids when she lunged at his head. It took a scolding, very strict monitoring, and several months for him to be at ease and reliable at Jeff and Michelle's.

But Homer eagerly bounded down the hall, into the living room, and hurtled right onto Michelle's lap. He licked her face furiously, then jumped over to the children and slobbered all over them, then Jeff. He even jumped down and licked Lulu. This more or less set the tone for Homer's approach to the new world.

Then he accompanied everyone upstairs for the kids' bedtime, hopping up on each of their beds for good-night kisses.

Meanwhile, Devon slipped off into the dining room to dump on the carpet.

❖❖❖❖❖❖❖❖❖

When we reached the cabin, I let both dogs out of the car and Devon took another lunge at Homer's head. Homer screamed, and so did I. Devon still looked outraged, far from compliant. Julius had been waiting for us and gave the puppy a warm greeting. Homer, no fool, loved him instantly and followed him everywhere. In fact, when we went out for a stroll, he walked half-underneath Julius, peering out at both me and Devon with nearly equal dread.

This wasn't as trouble-free as I'd hoped. Back inside, Homer came over to me gingerly, then froze. I looked over and saw Devon, crouched and ready to spring, giving him the herding eye. I chased Devon outside, then sat on the carpet and waited.

Homer, an adorable creature, crawled hesitantly into my lap and licked my hand as I scratched his belly and fed him some biscuits. Julius came over to console him, too; he had a profoundly generous spirit. Like Homer, Julius had known few conflicts and crises in his life. Loved and loving from birth, he was secure in his place in the world.

But he looked around warily for the Helldog. Good thing he didn't see what I saw on the other side of the sliding glass door—Devon's slim silhouette in the moonlight. He had never taken his eyes from Homer or from our scene of betrayal.

❖❖❖❖❖❖❖❖❖

Homer was different.

With Devon, life was still something of a brawl, punctuated by lengthening periods of calm, much loving, and some fun.

He had come far. He was sweet to people, happy working, walking, or riding with me, watching me, sticking his head out of a car window to catch the wind, chasing geese or trucks. He didn't mind accepting treats, compliments, or pats from admirers, and could be quite loving to his coterie of friends and admirers. But he was selective: everything else, he considered beneath his dignity.

He still challenged me, though less frequently. He did what I asked most of the time, but always in his own way, taking somewhat longer than necessary to come when I called, never lying down completely on the first request.

Homer—adjusting first to the cabin, then to New Jersey and all its attendant sounds and sights, unnerved by sirens and loud trucks and my bellowed commands at Devon—wanted no trouble. My yelling or throwing a choke chain—let alone a scooper— traumatized him. All he wanted was to know what I wanted. And to avoid incurring the displeasure of his hypervigilant elder brother.

I left Devon in the house for fifteen minutes or so twice a day and took Homer out alone for training sessions.

At first we worked in the front yard, until we both became aware of dark eyes glowering at us from an upstairs window. Then I took Homer to the park.

When we returned, Devon would always have found a way to show his pique. A couple of forks from the kitchen table would wind up deposited on the living-room sofa. I might find my shoes in a pile, their laces carefully removed, or sofa cushions pulled onto the floor, as if some gremlin had been rummaging through the house. The same old message: *Leave me behind and you'll pay. Every time.*

Devon had developed a genius for limits. He never destroyed or damaged any of the things he moved, nor did he ever get caught in the act of moving them. He was untouchable. Besides, his mischief wasn't serious, just a message—part of life with border collies. I could live with it. In fact, I think it annoyed him when I seemed not to notice.

But his response to Homer was a problem. Homer had stopped approaching me when I sat on the couch watching TV, and wouldn't jump up on the bed for a morning greeting. Yet when I walked over to pat or hug him, he wriggled and squealed for joy. Like Devon, he always wanted to keep me in sight, moving from room to room with me. But once there, he wouldn't leave his bed or sit by me for fear of Devon's malicious stare.

Deanne urged me to crack down. "It's not okay for him to keep Homer away from you," she warned. "It's *your* job to decide who can approach you."

Deanne said Devon was and always would be dominant, number two in the pack, after me, and as such had certain privileges: the right to eat first, for instance, or grab the best treats and rawhide chews and toys. Otherwise, I ought to call the shots.

At least Homer had an unambivalent adoration of Julius. They fell into a grandpa-grandson kind of relationship. When Devon glowered or snatched his toys, Homer would pout or retreat and curl up with Jules for comfort. They were devoted chums. But Julius was too gentle—or too above the fray—to defend his fuzzy little acolyte.

Sometimes the collies and I headed out and left Jules snoozing in the house or the yard, and returned two or three hours later to find him in the same position.

I wondered whether Jules was depressed. He was moving even less than usual. Perhaps he was still bereft at Stanley's loss. It hadn't been very long, really. In any case, I was terrified to take him to the vet. He seemed content.

So Devon and I went back to war over Homer. Homer stopped coming when I called, which was unacceptable and could be dangerous in a congested area. But when I put a leash on him and yanked him to me, and was voluble with praise and generous with treats when he complied, Devon was on us in a flash, crowding in jealously, once even nipping Homer and earning himself a swat with a rolled-up magazine. Once again, Devon displayed an awesome will and an independent mind, and a willingness to pay the price. I was his. Homer was welcome to stay in the house as long as he kept his distance.

In Devon's defense, Homer was an utterly adorable puppy who loved everybody, showering even total strangers with licks and nuzzles. He was still, at six months, small enough to scoop up in your arms, and sweet-tempered enough to be happy there. Devon, an obvious weirdo, elicited fewer coos and cuddles from passersby. He may have perceived his hard-won affection and attention as being in jeopardy again, and he was prepared to fight for it.

Swatting or yelling at Devon did no good in this tussle—it only scared Homer, who sensed when Devon and I were about to tangle, and fled. He hated it when Devon got into trouble, rushing over to lick him reassuringly. Homer was staunchly antiviolence. In fact, he was beginning to back away and hide when my training sessions began, or when I tried to brush him. If I gave in, Devon would be free to ignore all my commands, which was fine with him. If I insisted on being obeyed, I would risk traumatizing a new puppy.

New strategy: if Devon muscled in on Homer, or even looked menacing, I put him in the yard, where he couldn't see what was going on. This worked, sometimes. And Homer was a quick study.

We moved on to joint training sessions, so that Dev could show him what to do. I held a choke chain in my right hand and held my left hand up in the "stay" position, and as Devon moved two inches toward his kid brother, I tossed the chain at the floor in front of him. This scared the wits out of Homer at first, but he was pretty clever, too. It only took a week or two for him to recognize that Devon was getting yelled at, not him; that he was getting treats and Devon wasn't; that I would protect him.

So I watched him get easier, less intimidated around beta dog (to my alpha, of course), even more sociable. He was wary and honored the circle Devon drew around me, but day by day he lost his fear. When I called, he came wiggling and wagging to my side, a happy pup, though he never dallied long. He made friends in the neighborhood. He was Mr. Congeniality, much in the manner of Julius. We all reached a kind of truce, marked by some tension and wariness but less and less actual combat.

❖❖❖❖❖❖❖❖

It was becoming difficult, as winter loomed, to evade the fact that Julius was losing steam. He was following so far behind on our walks now that I sometimes walked him alone. Even then, he had lost interest in his deliberate sniffing. He seemed increasingly lifeless, eager to be with me, but not eager to leave the house. Even for a Lab as mellow as he was, something was off.

In December, full of foreboding and denial, I took him to the vet. We had another dreadful conversation—colon cancer, Dr. King said. Again I faced a set of grim choices, the unacceptably invasive or the questionably effective: surgery or chemotherapy. But it came down to the same decision. And to the same tile floor, the same goodbye hugs. Jules slurped Dr. King and her assistant as they gave him the injections. "Jerk," I said shakily, cradling his big head in my lap. "Stop licking them. Don't you know they're killing you?"

Stroking his head, trying not to lose control and frighten him, I told Julius quietly that if there was such a place as heaven, he had definitely made the cut.

It would be a mountaintop where he could lie happily and gaze out over a meadow. Lots of wildflowers, I told him, so he'd have lovely things to sniff without even having to get up. The sun would shine always. A pile of rawhide chips smeared with peanut butter would be within easy reach and would never diminish.

In the meadow below, a parade of foxes, rabbits, deer, and raccoons would pass by for his amusement but—a special feature of Julius's paradise—a river would flow between him and them, so he wouldn't feel any pressure to chase them or even respond, but he would feel free to contemplate life and meditate upon its mysteries.

Plus, children. Hordes of the little kids he loved so much. They'd line up for a few hours each day, kids who were sick, who'd been bitten by lesser dogs, who feared dogs, who were meeting their first dog up close. They'd step up hesitantly, clutching their parents' hands, and he'd lean over the way he always did, very slowly, no sudden moves, and give them gentle slurps on their cheeks. "Nice doggie," the moms and dads would say, as they always did, guiding chubby hands down his sleek white coat and across his magnificent head.

The kids would hug him and love him, and all dogs, for all time.

I told him that Stanley would be there too, the team reunited, companions forever, Stanley with an endless supply of sticks and twigs to pile up here and there in secret places.

Me, I told him honestly, I wasn't so sure about; I wasn't as generous or as loving as my Labs. But Julius would know peace. And somewhere during this mumbled, faltering account, he quietly slipped away.

Afterwards, my daughter, Emma, called home to ask how I was. "There's a big hole in my heart, and I think I'll never fill it," I told her. I found myself choking up at odd times of the day, at my computer or in the car, and early in the morning when I looked over at the dog bed in the corner and Jules was not there.

People ask me if I knew, perhaps unconsciously, that Stanley or Julius was ailing before I took in Devon and Homer. The truth is, I don't know. Anyone over fifty who's paying attention has a heightened sense of mortality. I was extremely sensitive to the Labs, who as a breed don't have great longevity; perhaps without quite realizing it, I'd noticed that each of them was changing, slowing down. Perhaps that spurred me to bring home Devon and Homer.

But consciously, the idea of either Lab dying soon hadn't entered my mind. I thought they would be with us for several years, at least, showing the newcomers how it was done, introducing them to favorite haunts upstate, monitoring the increasing household. I thought in the summer that Stanley might give swimming lessons in the Battenkill. The way it worked out, the coming and going, was symmetrical but premature.

I returned to a two-dog household once more. Devon looked around for Julius sometimes, but to be frank, he always appreciated less competition for my attention. Homer seemed lost. I saw him trotting through the house, searching for his companion. It comforted him, I think, to climb into my lap; certainly it comforted me. It was the first real bond we shared; mourning brought us closer. And he began padding around after Devon, who, I noticed, would bestow on him the occasional morning lick. The Three Amigos had, somewhat sadly, re-formed.

Eleven

POULTRYGEIST

---

*L*ike other friends and loved ones, dogs can mark periods in one's life, boundaries between one time and another.

Julius and Stanley were my dogs during the years when I left behind media companies and big commercial institutions and became a solitary writer. They were by my side when I wrote nearly all my books, articles, and columns. They were around for much of my daughter's childhood. Almost all my ideas germinated or developed while I was walking them. For a socially uneasy man, they provided real companionship; not a replacement for human beings, but a steadfast and loving presence. They offered gifts I could never repay.

When a dog like Devon enters your life, your days become so full that it's easy to let the memory of those warm, undemanding creatures fade away. Devon took up space; he made everyone around him take notice. It was a blessing and a curse.

Life with him is a curious mix of love and fun and an intellectual combat that never entirely ends. His is just not a pliant personality.

For instance: a couple of months after Homer arrived, Paula and I came home from a movie to find the refrigerator door standing ajar. Conspicuously missing: the roast chicken I'd bought at the supermarket, encased in a domed plastic tray that was hard to pry open. Hmmm . . . someone had goofed and neglected to close the door properly, and someone else had taken full advantage of the goof. I had a fair idea who.

I looked around the kitchen and saw no chicken. I did see Devon scurrying up the stairs so silently I would have missed it if I hadn't glimpsed his disappearing tail. Homer, always stricken at the prospect of trouble, had the panicky look that came on him whenever Devon and I tangled. And by now, I believed Devon was capable of almost any kind of mischief.

Something was definitely afoot. I gave the dining room and family room careful scrutiny. Nothing. But something was sticking out from beneath a black leather chair in the living room. It was the bottom half of the plastic container, but there wasn't a shred of chicken in it.

Crawling around the room, I located the other half underneath the sofa. Neither part of the container had been chewed or torn, simply opened with the dexterity that usually requires an opposable thumb.

I yelled to Paula in her office. "Is Devon up there with you?"

"Yes," she said, pleased. "He came up to visit me, which he hardly ever does when you're around. He looks nervous."

It took me a few days to piece it together, and even then I wasn't sure what had happened. The chicken had weighed several pounds. How could a dog, even finding the refrigerator providentially open, pull the chicken out, carry it twenty-five feet without dropping it or making a stain, pry open a plastic container, eat every scrap without leaving a trace, then stash the evidence under two different pieces of furniture? It didn't add up, even for legendarily crafty border collies.

Too many steps, too much calculation. Still, whatever had happened had happened; I could hardly yell at him after the fact. Besides, I still didn't quite believe it.

The chicken's fate, however accomplished, was clear when we took our walk that night. Devon had gorged himself; the weakness in his plan was that with a dog, what goes in soon comes out. From the evidence, Homer probably hadn't gotten a morsel. Knowing that eating poultry bones could be dangerous, I called Dr. King, who told me to watch for any bleeding. And to be sure to close the fridge when I left the house.

Two days later, I bought some meatballs in a similar container for lunch and put them in the refrigerator. And, yes, I made sure the door was closed and slid a kitchen chair in front of it for good measure. When I came up from my office an hour later, the chair was askew, the refrigerator open, the meatballs gone. I found the container underneath the black leather chair. Devon was edging toward the stairs.

This time, I roared, picking up the container and yelling "No!" Charging after Devon, I tripped over the carpet, sprawling to the floor. Homer shrieked. Devon was nowhere to be found.

I e-mailed Deanne. Had she ever known a border collie to open a refrigerator? "Only one," she replied. "Devon's mom."

This was a whole new level of trouble, something that would drive me mad. I hated the idea of guarding food from a sneaky dog.

What particularly bothered me was that Devon didn't really care much about food.

He picked and nibbled at his own, hardly ever finishing it at one sitting, sometimes forgetting about it altogether. We'd known for months that he could open the kitchen cabinet that held the big sacks of dog food. But he never actually ate it when we were away. Dog food? Where was the challenge in that?

This stunt, similarly, had little to do with hunger. It was either pique at being left—my bet—or one of those games border collies come up with to occupy themselves when they're bored. Opening a sealed refrigerator with your nose (I guess) and then opening a snapped-together plastic container (How? I couldn't imagine)—now *that* was fun.

I was upset. Devon had been doing so well. There was a malevolent quality to this, I thought.

Paula, on the other hand, was rather impressed. She started talking about hiding the car keys, the credit cards, and computer passwords.

Another fight. I was a veteran by now, with many scars, battle ribbons, and stories to tell of my campaigns.

I bought some turkey burgers at the market, tucked them into the fridge, put my coat on, and went out into the backyard.

Wishing I had a video camera—a collie-cam—that would record and reveal exactly how the hell this theft was going down, I stood perfectly still, my ear to the door. A couple of minutes later, I heard what I thought was a very light thud, and charged inside.

There, sitting on the floor of the family room, was the popped-open container, the turkey burgers still inside. The refrigerator door stood open. Homer was paralyzed with fear and Devon had beat a tactical retreat.

How dare he? I girded for battle, until a lightbulb went off in my head and I reminded myself of certain verities. Paula was right. It was both amusing and impressive. And he's a border collie. He's Devon, the Professor Moriarty of dogs. If you love him, accept him. This is part of life with him.

I laughed and sat down on the floor. "Hey, boy," I said to Homer, who rushed over, immensely relieved and full of kisses. "C'mon down, Devon, you creep," I yelled upstairs. "It's okay." Devon came roaring down a second later, knocking Homer out of the way and landing in my lap. We hugged for a while, the bewildered but overjoyed Homer trying to get into the act.

What can you do but laugh and sigh and accept the new nature of things? It wasn't easy, because of all the impatience and anger and frustration in my life, and because I so missed Julius and Stanley and their peaceful reliability. But it was necessary, because I was so crazy about this deranged dog.

"You know what?" I said. "For all that ingenuity, you deserve the burger." I took it out of the leakproof plastic, put one turkey patty in Homer's bowl and one in Devon's. Homer scarfed it up gleefully, but Devon didn't touch his, glancing at it with disdain. The thrill was purely in the hunt.

❖❖❖❖❖❖❖❖❖

This was another turning point in my tempestuous relationship with the Helldog, and it was a healthy one for me. Devon was going to be Devon; I could take it hard and make us all nuts, or I could take it easy.

Still, I wasn't about to let him chow down on our dinner, nor was I going to roll over. I went to my computer, logged on to a search engine, and ordered a set of childproofing locks for appliances, to be shipped overnight.

I also posted this latest adventure on a border collie Web site, where it inspired a general round of can-you-top-this comments. Stealing a chicken was nothing, apparently. One woman from Ohio wrote that her border collie opened cabinets and feasted on maple syrup.

"All this time," one of my fellow border collie owners e-mailed me, "he's been watching to see where the food comes from. He's been paying attention. It's a *gotcha*."

Yeah, maybe, but his owner was no fool, either. Next day, I secured the fridge with the child lock and went out, giving Devon the finger.

When I came home, the refrigerator's bottom grill had been knocked off. Having failed to open the door, Devon had tried to dig in through the bottom.

✦✦✦✦✦✦✦✦✦

And he hung in there for a while. We put the bottom grill back on; it was off when we came home. We took it off and left it off. I know it's beneath me, but once in a while, when Paula isn't around, I point to the refrigerator lock and jeer at him. "Gotcha back," I yell.

I also got two dog crates, covered the tops with quilts, and built a cozy, calming cave for Homer and Devon, stocked with water, rawhide, and marrow bones. Let Devon be Devon, but let him learn to love and use the crate every now and then, too. They both quickly came to love short stays inside their little dens—rushing inside happily—and Paula and I could venture out in peace. With Devon, I'd learned, it was always smart to deny him the opportunity to make mischief. He'd rather come along, but failing that, he seemed relieved to have a haven.

When Julius and Stanley passed beyond puppyhood, they reached a Zen-like state of grace marked by evenness, gentleness, an almost obsessive regularity. Life stopped changing for them. Their reliability was one of their great qualities.

For Devon, every day is a new experience, as it now is for me. His love and loyalty are beyond question; it sometimes appears that he has submitted.

But to conclude that he's lost interest—in the refrigerator, in figuring out how things work, in sticking it to me now and then—would be a big mistake. He is always waiting, watching.

Twelve

DOG DAYS

A day with Devon and Homer begins at about six-thirty A.M., which is when I open my eyes. Devon is always—always—sitting on the floor a few feet from the bed, watching, awaiting my signal.

I wave my hand, and he hops quietly—so as not to wake Paula—onto the bed next to me. He puts his head on my right shoulder, licks my hand or face. Then he sighs deeply, and goes to sleep.

It is our time together, inviolate, just him and me, contented. Perhaps he's recollecting our early struggles, and sharing the same sense of relief I feel.

Sometime before Paula's alarm goes off, at seven-thirty, Homer stirs, yawns, gets up, and approaches the bed from the opposite corner. Keeping a wary eye on Devon, who still tracks his every move, he wriggles quietly up onto the bed between Paula and me. He is a serious cuddler, nestling into any available spot.

For months, Devon enforced a no-fly zone around me. But he never kept Homer away from Paula; consequently, the two have fallen in love. Sometimes I look over to see him wrapped around her head like a fluffy turban.

Though they're first cousins, Homer and Devon occupy opposite ends of the border collie spectrum. Homer has no defiance or dominance in him; unless a chipmunk or squirrel appears on the horizon, he's all sweetness and frolic.

He learns commands quickly. Within a week of his arrival, he was housebroken, able to walk off-leash and sit, heel, lie down (always the toughest), and stay. Yelling at him was counterproductive and unnecessary; the kinds of battles I had fought with Devon would have crushed Homer. Once you show him what you want, he does it cheerfully.

He's a perfectly wonderful dog—obedient, bright, and good-tempered. Deanne was quite right: these two have evolved into a great pair.

As she promised, Homer is pleased to be the underdog, which is fortunate, since Devon insists upon it. Devon gets to decide who chews what; he always walks up front; he has dibs on me. That's all fine with Homer. He's managed to love us, and be much loved by us, without ever putting Devon out of joint, threatening, or supplanting him. He's slipped easily into our lives. He and I are still working out the nature of our relationship, but I can't recall a single problem he's caused, apart from an understandable fetish for Paula's sheepskin slippers.

Devon understands me well, and connects with my darker side; Homer doesn't seem to have one.

We all go downstairs for breakfast—each dog, I am proud to report, eating from his own bowl, no minor or quickly won accomplishment. Devon gets fed first, his dominance respected. Once in a while if Devon's feeling malignant, he'll knock Homer away and grab a chunk or two of his food before I back him off, but he seems to do that largely to annoy me, and to protect his reputation.

They then go lie in the hallway, waiting for their walk, while Paula and I talk, read the paper, drink coffee. The dogs, intuitive creatures, understand that this is our time.

But the scraping of my chair as I back away from the table is their signal to jump up, nose open the door to the rear hallway, and sit by the back door. The sound of my zipping up a jacket can send Devon into expectant barks as he eagerly looks toward the door.

Border collies don't merely exit—they explode. They fly out the door as if shot from cannons, looking for backyard rodents or passing commuters, circling the yard until they are satisfied that things are in order.

Then I simply announce the direction in which we're walking. I've gotten used to chatting with these dogs now; it seems only natural to explain where we're headed.

❖❖❖❖❖❖❖❖❖

With my encouragement, Devon has retired from vehicle-chasing. Too risky. Too hard to control. Too easy for him to misinterpret a hand signal and get flattened. So Devon, with his usual ingenuity, has perfected the car-less chase.

Each morning, we walk to a half-mile strip of grass alongside the high school athletic field, where Devon drops into the crouch. On my command—"Go get 'em"—he stampedes down the fenced strip, then pivots and runs back. He's not chasing anything in particular; it's herding without the herd. I don't know if Devon envisions sheep or trucks, or if he fixates on some sound or sight invisible to me, but he has a blast, running himself ragged, and taking the whole matter with complete seriousness. By the time we reach the end of the strip, his tongue is hanging from one side of his mouth and he is a tired and happy border collie. His atavistic Hemp-ish instincts satisfied, he's quite calm.

Every now and then I renew my promise that one day I'll take him to a sheep farm, let him experience the real thing.

❖❖❖❖❖❖❖❖❖

Our neighborhood walks have grown almost ceremonial in their complexity now. People pull over in cars to remark on Devon and Homer, though not quite as often as they did for Julius and Stanley.

Devon would be just as content to ignore his public; Homer, however, does enough schmoozing for both of them. He has a gaggle of human and canine admirers who greet him, carry biscuits in case they encounter him, want to play with him. If I'm not disciplined, it can take quite a while to traverse the block.

In the process, he's coaxed Devon and me, who both have antisocial streaks, to be more gregarious, to spend time with people, to make friends. As good-hearted as the Labs were, Homer is markedly more outgoing: he'll spot a total stranger sitting on a porch and bound over, tail going, ready to offer slurps. He now knows where every one of his dog pals lives and pauses at their driveways to whoof a greeting. Often, the dog comes shooting out, followed by its owner and their children. The dogs then wrestle around in a blurry ball, so spirited that Homer often limps home with sprains. We keep buffered aspirin on hand.

At first reluctantly, Devon and I have begun to join in this spirit of happy trekking. We will never be as friendly or as open as Homer, but he's softened us up, pulled us out of ourselves. We've met neighbors whose names I didn't know; I've had long, intimate chats with people I'd never spoken with. After six months with Homer, I feel more connected to my block, know more people, can discuss kids, the schools, all the staples of suburban conversation.

I've been touched, too, by the interest in and concern for Devon. My neighbors, some of whom had been witnesses to our brawling past, rooted for Devon from the first. They still make it a point to greet and pet him, to ask after him and comment on his relaxed demeanor. They're his support group; mine, too.

✦✦✦✦✦✦✦✦

Our neighborhood has some of the nicest, best-behaved dogs you could wish for. A few are boisterous after spending their days alone and confined. But in general I think of our street as a model of the happy place dogs can still occupy, even in our challenging contemporary world.

Everybody carries bags and scoopers and cleans up. Everyone's made sure to socialize their dogs early on, with other dogs and with kids and adults. The dogs know how to play, but they also know how to pay attention. I've come to see that this isn't a matter of individual wizardry; it comes from time, and from tedious and responsible training.

I like to credit the spirit of Julius and Stanley for some of this. They were so well loved that their exemplary behavior and good natures convinced most of my neighbors to hire Ralph Fabbo as their dogs' trainer. It pays off.

Homer has a social life that I'll never come close to attaining. Dog owners all over the block call for playdates.

He's tight with Zeus, a German shepherd three times his

size; and Seamus, a tiny, energetic Westie; and Daisy, a curly-haired retriever. He's become very close to Minnie, the deaf pit bull he meets at a nearby park.

But his main squeeze is Lucy, the black standard poodle who lives across the street. Sometimes, early in the morning or at dusk, they can be heard barking at each other, sending secret signals.

Between visits, as we walk, Homer noses my pants pocket, where I keep Stanley's old blue ball, now entering its second generation of service. I toss it whenever we come to an open field. Homer loves to chase, though he isn't crazy about retrieving. Devon disdains such foolishness, except when Homer's having too much fun. Then he'll grab the ball away and bring it to me, his way of letting me know that he *could* perform this stunt but doesn't consider it worth his time.

These strolls are complex; we zigzag all over the neighborhood, back and forth across the streets, making a kind of obedience trial of the walk, just to keep the boys interested. I give them the heads up—"Hey, guys, pay attention"—and check the traffic, then point to the spot across the street where I want them to go. "Let's go, heel" is the command to tear across at high speeds, straight to the other side, to the opposite corner, or on a diagonal. "Heel slowly" means to trot calmly alongside me as I cross.

We walk through shady streets, neighborhood shopping districts, in and around parks and schools. At the invitation of exasperated township officials, we sometimes clear geese out of playgrounds and parks.

I carry leashes in my jacket pocket in case we need to reassure a nervous jogger or show a cop our ability to comply with the letter of the law. But we rarely need them. The gentlemen are good walkers now, happy to take in the sights, stretch their legs, keep me company.

After the morning walk, it's time for work.

I write every day and many evenings, and my dogs understand their side of the contract. Devon and Homer have come to grasp the meaning of the computer's booting up. It's when we go our separate ways.

If it's a pleasant day, I open the back door and shoo them out. A parental instinct: they should be outside chasing squirrels, not sitting in a basement study with a sedentary man.

But on nasty days, they have a choice. They're free to bunk down in my study, which is, of course, fully equipped with dog beds and rawhide. I'm surprised at how often they opt to lie on the floor beside me while I write. Homer likes to doze with his head on my shoe.

Sometimes, though, they do leave me to my keyboard and go off elsewhere in the house. Knowing Devon, I figure he's upstairs studying German or assembling a giant LEGO installation. Or maybe he's training innocent Homer in the black arts of opening refrigerator doors and removing shoelaces. I don't really know; I'm working.

In the late afternoon, when I'm ready to stop, we do chores.

I take Homer and Devon almost everyplace. They come with me to the neighborhood copy shop, curling up on the floor and awaiting customers. In my tolerant town, they've met my barber, a local car dealer, the florist, and the dry cleaner, and visited the camera store and the picture-framing shop.

It's odd about these dogs: outside, they have boundless energy, but when I bring them inside, they plop down and cool out. In Britain, my border collie books report, sheepherders often bring their dogs into pubs, where they nap under the tables. Pubs are a custom we ought to import. Instead, Homer and Devon trot into the bookstore, wait patiently while I browse or chat, allow children to hug them.

When I can't bring them inside, I leave them in the car (warm days excepted) with the windows open a crack. When I return, our reunions are as joyous as if I'd just returned from a few months in Borneo.

The dogs—at least Homer—don't mind being left alone so much anymore, though; they have each other for company. I sometimes look out my office window into the backyard and see the two of them sitting side by side, waiting for a misguided rodent to take one step onto their turf, like old friends for whom fishing is mostly an excuse to sit on a riverbank together.

Evenings, since we have no access to animal-friendly pubs and I can't sneak dogs into restaurants or movie theaters, Paula and I often go out.

Sometimes I leave them out of the crate. And every time I do leave Devon and Homer alone and free in the house, I still find innocuous messages when I come back—the video cabinet open, sofa pillows on the floor, CD cases on the bed. We still keep the refrigerator locked.

Days with them are busy and satisfying—play and work, love and exercise. I write a lot, walk a lot. I get licked a lot; I scratch ears a lot. I throw the ball and distribute rawhide and the occasional squeaky toy. I have companions, sidekicks, co-conspirators.

❖❖❖❖❖❖❖❖❖

The cabin upstate is even better; it's border collie heaven. When I start loading up the Trooper, Homer and Devon surround me, circling. Devon has more than once tried to climb into my duffel bag; he knows what it means the second I take it from the closet.

The dogs have the backseat, covered in old quilts and blankets, to themselves. They take in the scenery while I keep the radio tuned to Yankees' games. It takes four hours to get to our place, and once I'm off the interstates, I roll the back windows down a little. The boys like to sniff the air.

As we drive up the mountain road, Devon starts barking. I open the door when we reach the cabin, and the dogs shoot out into the woods and take a few laps around the meadow.

One of the gifts these two have brought me is a passion for hiking and walking—coinciding, unfortunately, with the advent of a bum ankle. When I had good feet, I disliked hiking. But border collie owners can't survive very long as couch potatoes.

So the first thing we do when we arrive upstate is set off on a stroll through the woods behind the cabin. If we've timed it right, we can catch the sun setting behind the hills.

Julius and Stanley liked to walk, and I remember those walks happily. They were peaceful affairs, but they didn't last long. Bugs and flies, heat and cold got to the Labs; they were always eager to saunter home again after fifteen minutes or so.

Devon and Homer, however, are perpetual-motion machines. Bugs don't bother them. Weather has no effect, either. They have astonishing agility, bobbing and weaving, darting under and over and around logs, trees, streams. And they are alert to every wild turkey, field mouse, and monarch butterfly in the vicinity.

Their awareness has heightened my own, and the walks are lovely in a completely different way. These guys have made me more conscious of what's in these woods, have induced me to pay attention, to share their enthusiasm for whatever they see. Homer and Devon are alive in a visceral way. Their vitality is infectious, perhaps my favorite thing about the breed. They are alive down to the tip of their tails. They've turned me—even me—into an outdoorsman of sorts.

On the mountaintop, we get up at five or six A.M. and head out on our first hike. I bring a Thermos of hot coffee, a cell phone in case I fall down once too often, and the usual cache of biscuits.

Sometimes we work across the big meadow behind the house; sometimes we muscle through the high snow. Sometimes we just amble along our dirt road, Homer racing after the ball as it careens down the hill.

Since there are few streets and even fewer cars, they are really free when we're at the cabin, and they know it. Devon's flight through the woods the first time he came up seems eons ago. He never strays far. I don't need leashes, scoopers, commands. They just go, keeping me more or less in sight as they fly, and I beam like a dad whose kids are having the time of their lives.

Upstate, Homer's charms have worked to make Devon more playful, too, though he only reveals this when no one else is around.

Homer takes off through the fields or around the house. At first, Devon had no problem running him down, but Homer is bigger and wilier now. As Devon bears down, Homer vanishes into the trees or the tall meadow grass, reappearing every few minutes to bark tauntingly, then disappear again. His eyes have a demonic gleam. After months of being pushed around, this is his revenge, and it seems sweet.

Devon tears after him wildly. But Homer pops up every-where, like a figure in a video game. Once in a while Devon con-nects, grabs him by the collar, and throws him to the ground. Homer goes limp, waits till Devon eases up, then bolts. They could do this for hours. Over the course of a day, they do. It gives me so much pleasure to watch that I often surprise myself by laughing out loud.

In between, we go back to the cabin so I can write. By night-fall, we are all exhausted. Homer and Devon settle in for an hour or two of serious rawhide chewing while I crank up a fire and set-tle in with a book. Evenings are peaceful: a blaze in the fireplace, a good book or a baseball game in season, a bottle of scotch on the table, a dog on either side of my chair. They finally quit by ten o'clock, and sometime after that I climb into bed and turn off the bedroom light.

After a few minutes, I'm conscious of a light, feathery pres-ence to the left of my head—that would be the nimble Devon, claiming the other pillow, and then a few moments later, Homer's quick hop onto the foot of the bed. We all pretend to be follow-ing the rules, which are that dogs aren't supposed to spend the night on the bed.

On howling, bitter winter nights, however, the three of us

drop all pretense; we become a pack and climb in and curl up together at the top of the world, the Three Amigos staving off the
Furies.

❖❖❖❖❖❖❖❖❖

We are in great harmony, though of a different kind. Life with
these dogs is never simple, and rarely as relaxed as it was with
Julius and Stanley. But we are such a trio now, so easy and calm
together, and we have so much fun, that I already have some trouble recollecting those first weeks and months. Even when I'm
back in New Jersey, where almost every morning we pass the
street-corner battlefield on which Devon and I had our fiercest
confrontation, it feels like another lifetime. Is this sleek, proud,
quiet dog the same one who shattered windows, charged buses,
leaped onto passing minivans? People shock me by praising his
calmness. But it's true, I rarely yell at Devon now; I haven't
needed to.

I'm still learning, though. A well-bred, good-hearted Labrador gives his allegiance freely, without conditions. A border collie needs reason to support his faith. Julius did what I asked of
him because, quite simply, his work was to please me. He required no explanations or elaboration.

Devon is different: he wants to know why. You can't just bark
commands and expect him to blindly obey. You have to provide
coherence and rationale, persuade this instinctively independent

dog that there's a point. Otherwise he feels demeaned, like a circus performer. And that leads to trouble.

So there are strings attached, conditions set, and it's this intellectual process, this challenge, that forms a bond or breaks it. Contrary to myth, the connection isn't automatic. In fact, it's one of the risks of having a dog like this, perhaps one reason the breed is so often abandoned. Border collies make choices. The relationship can fail, can become tense and laden.

But how lucky I am to have found this again. Once more, I have two wonderful dogs whom I love dearly, who love me back. I can't shake the sense that I've witnessed something both commonplace and important, comings and goings that aren't just metaphors for life, but life itself.

Sitting near Julius's upstate spot, I tend to think back on what I've lost and gained in the year since Devon arrived. My daughter went back to college, as she should, taking a chunk of my soul with her. My mother died. Some friends drifted away. I lost the full use of my left leg. And I lost Julius and Stanley. Big holes in my heart, all of them.

Yet when I think about that time, I see more gain than loss. I think of a great marriage that absorbs disruption but endures, of a wonderful daughter making her way toward independence, of work that I cherish, and two more magnificent animals to distract me from my woes, give me new ways to nurture, and love me purely and powerfully and without complication.

Thirteen

BARBIE COLLIES

As a suburban dad driving a Volvo and then a minivan, a proud Boomer parent ferrying my "gifted and talented" daughter from art class to guitar lessons, I'd acquired a local nickname—"The Prince of Rides."

So it was no great surprise to anybody who knew me that on a crisp day in April 2001, I was cruising to eastern Pennsylvania with Homer and Devon to fulfill their potential.

We were headed for Raspberry Ridge Farm to meet Carolyn Wilki, a Bryn Mawr– and Cornell-educated animal behaviorist and psychologist and onetime corporate executive who is to herding what a kung fu master is to aspiring martial artists. And we were going to encounter some sheep, as I'd promised Devon we would one day.

I had heard a lot about Wilki and her farm. She was a dog mystic, a student of the canine psyche, a specialist in dog training and aggression, whispered about in obedience classes and on Web sites devoted to herding dogs. She was rumored to be a gifted but eccentric trainer, unorthodox, demanding yet successful. She could, it was said, see into a dog's soul.

❖❖❖❖ ❖ ❖❖❖❖

Wilki taught dogs by praising them when they did right—a growing training philosophy called positive reinforcement.

She built dogs up, never shouted at them or humiliated them, teaching them by showing what they were doing right, not by scolding, yelling, or throwing chains. She had, it was said, no patience for people who mistreated their dogs, or power-tripped, or overindulged them in Boomer fashion. If you and your dogs passed her qualifying test, the ancient, mythic world of herding was open to you. If you didn't, you were out, licking your wounds and sulking like a parent whose kid didn't get into the right college.

My dogs were excited, staring expectantly out the windows, and so was I. Something clearly was up.

"Gentlemen, this is the first day of the rest of your lives," I had announced in the morning, as Devon trumpeted the first of several enthusiastic *roo*'s to get us launched on this fascinating day. (For a border collie, every new day is fascinating.) "You're going to meet your destiny!"

Little Homer was growing up, losing some of his shyness and caution and demonstrating a breathtaking athletic ability, unprecedented for anyone in my family. Still lighter and smaller than Devon, his agility was amazing. He dove into ponds, caught mice on the run, once pulled a hapless sparrow right out of the air, could dodge any foe and run for hours with his pals. He deserved a chance to see what he could do with some livestock, too.

❖❖❖❖❖❖❖❖

Devon yelped once or twice with excitement as we pulled into Raspberry Ridge, making our way down a winding gravel road toward a stone barn with huge fenced corrals on either side. We could hear sheep baaing somewhere, a sound that caused both dogs' ears to stand up.

An American border collie—shorthaired, lean, a bit homely, businesslike—popped out of the barn to check us out. It wasn't a casual inspection. Dave—we were later introduced—was part of the reception team.

He was older, grizzled, not the sort to be bathed in avocado shampoo or otherwise coddled. This, I thought, was probably more or less what the ancient Romans had in mind when they trained dogs to herd sheep. Dave looked at me, cast a glance at my well-groomed lads with their flowing coats and full bellies, gave a very perfunctory wag, and pivoted back toward the barn.

The herding-dog world, I knew, was fiercely divided. The pet breeders believed that border collies could herd but still be great family companions. The herding camp was understandably terrified that the breed was about to be mass-marketed and cosseted out of existence, losing its ancient role and instincts.

Dave was the herding sort. Homer and Devon seemed respectful of him—no playing, sniffing, or herding. Back at the barn, he summoned Carolyn Wilki.

She strode our way, a thin woman in her late thirties, I guessed, wearing a suede slouch hat and a bemused expression, carrying a crook and dressed in an army-fatigue jacket. She seemed to me to have stepped out of Devonshire, perhaps by way of the outback. She was soft-spoken and direct, without much small talk.

"This is Dave," she said, gesturing to her assistant. He ambled over to my side, sniffing at my backpack, which held a plastic bag filled with biscuits.

"Can I give him one?" I asked Carolyn, after shaking her hand and introducing myself.

"Sure," she said. "He'll love you for it."

I tossed Dave a liver treat, which he stared at incredulously and inhaled. Then he rolled over on his back and licked my shoes.

Carolyn eyed the dogs appraisingly, then eyed me. Her manner was friendly, but skeptical. "Can I ask you something?" she said. "Why are you here?"

I wasn't sure what she meant.

"We don't get many Barbie collies," she replied. It hardly sounded like a compliment.

"Barbie collies?"

"Well, show dogs. We don't get many. They usually don't have much herding instinct left; it's been bred out of them. So I was just wondering why you brought them all the way out here, why you've come."

This seemed familiar. I was picturing the day, a couple of years back, when I paced outside a university admissions building while my daughter had her interview inside. This interrogation generated the same odd feeling in my stomach.

It was a fair question, though. This wasn't a likely place for me to be. I wasn't sad to leave behind the years of driving my charges to lessons, and Homer and Devon seemed to be doing just fine without sheep in their lives. But I had made a promise, and I'd very much wanted to come.

I took my time answering. "It's a question of honor," I finally said.

Dave, nosing at my backpack for another biscuit, had sat down to listen.

"What do you mean?" Carolyn said, leaning on her crook. It was a gorgeous spring day, the breeze stirring the dogs' fur.

I explained the promise. "And besides, I owe it to them, I guess," I said. "These are wonderful dogs. They're good to me and I really love them and I want, if only for half an hour, to let them come face-to-face with what they have been bred to do for centuries. Just once, they ought to get to do their work. They ought to herd some sheep. Does that sound strange?"

I watched her alert, no-nonsense face. If she didn't think it would work, there'd be no messing around: we'd be out of there. Herding was intense, she'd warned me over the phone, even mildly dangerous.

Carolyn nodded. "That's a good answer," she said. "But Barbie collies . . ."

Well, I humphed—nobody was going to dis my dogs—these were Australian dogs, by way of Texas, and I'd been led to believe that their herding instinct was intact.

"Oh, really?" she said amiably.

I could only imagine how Deanne would erupt when I reported this. She thought some of the herding partisans were plain fanatics, breeding needlessly hostile, undomesticated dogs.

But Dave, calm and prepared as a suburban driving instructor confronting yet another terrified teenager, looked ready for a go. He was clearly in favor of our sticking around. I tossed him another biscuit—having an ally couldn't hurt.

For the next fifteen minutes, Homer and Devon and I watched while Dave and Carolyn moved some sheep from the barn into a holding pen, then down a long path and into a fenced pasture.

Carolyn was patient with the sheep, occasionally whipping out her crook and pulling a lamb from the flock. She wanted to separate the babies and select some veterans who wouldn't be frightened by frenzied new dogs, although she clearly didn't foresee much of a threat.

Dave had shifted into herding mode, picking up on her choices and commands, keeping the sheep moving, circling them again and again, doggedly and patiently, while she culled the ranks. It was a seamless operation.

I looked up the hill and saw several trucks and cars parked up on the ridge, people stopping to watch. Something about this ancient practice was still captivating.

One dog at a time in the pasture, Carolyn said, when she had everything satisfactorily arranged. For the well-being of the sheep and the safety of all. Safety?

Furthermore, she cautioned, it was important that I watch the sheep, not the dogs. "If they come for you, turn sideways; usually they'll part around you," she said casually. "If you feel them crashing into your legs, go down. Better to break a leg than blow out a knee." Wait. Who'd said anything about my going in there? I had to interact with sheep?

Carolyn smiled. Of course, she said. The instinct test wasn't just for the dogs, and herding wasn't, either.

Somehow, I'd pictured Carolyn doing the instructing; I'd be outside the corral, beaming. I didn't have much experience with livestock, no old instincts to draw on.

Besides, the pasture was filled with half a dozen twitchy sheep and their plentiful droppings, and if Carolyn was skeptical of us, the sheep looked even more suspicious. They were bigger and meaner looking than you might think. I already had a bad leg, and I had no desire for blown knees *or* broken bones.

But there was no way I would walk away from this odyssey now. Confirm every prejudice about Barbie collies and their wimpy owners? Disappoint my now keenly interested guys? Break my word to Devon that, if he didn't die under the wheels of a school bus, we would someday meet some sheep?

I should chain Devon to a post a short distance from the pasture, Carolyn advised. The sheep would have enough to deal with, between me, Dave, and Homer. They didn't need another cranked-up border collie on patrol. And stand away from the gates, she added. They could become "hot spots" if things got rough.

I suddenly wanted to go home. But something had switched

on inside Dev and Homer. They were more keyed up than I had ever seen them, which is saying something. Obsessed with what Dave was doing, their heads had been swiveling like spectators' at a fast-paced tennis match. They were totally absorbed in the herding, the connection between the dog, the herder, and the sheep; the rest of the world seemed to dematerialize.

As if this were something they had seen before, and were ready for, they tensed; their eyes widening. Even their physical posture changed. They seemed so alert that I thought they might explode.

I chained Devon to the post and brought the leashed Homer into the pasture, latching the gate behind us.

"Remember," Carolyn called, "watch the sheep, not the dogs." She ran through the herding commands and terms for me, illustrating with Dave: "fetch" to drive the sheep to her; "gather" for the dog to collect the sheep into a compact group; "go bye" for the dog to circle to the left of the sheep; "way to me," for the dog to reverse his direction and circle to the right. "Steady" was the command for the dog to slow to a creeping walk. Of course, the celebrated "that'll do" (as in the movie *Babe*) released the dog from his work.

The moment of truth.

"Unleash him," she said. Homer took off as if from a launching pad, right for Dave and the sheep bleating nervously fifty yards away. You'd think he'd done this a hundred times. He ran to the opposite side of the herd, across from Dave, and started lunging here, then there, circling the sheep, joining Dave as Carolyn issued a stream of commands.

Dave clearly had this drill down pat. Calm, efficient, he could move the sheep by eyeing them, moving first in one direction, then in the other, looping back to collect strays, then retreating to a far corner to await instructions. Homer, meanwhile, was no longer recognizable as the cutie who crawled onto Paula's pillow every morning. He was a fiend, charging, barking, nipping, occasionally emerging from the herd with a mouthful of wool.

"Wow," Carolyn said. "He's a champ." Homer, she announced, was using every tactic in the border collie repertoire—his body, his teeth, the "eye." Behind me, I heard Devon barking furiously and pulling at the leash.

I was mesmerized, until Carolyn yelled in alarm, "Watch the sheep! Watch the sheep!" I looked up as five or six of them—Homer in hot pursuit—whirled around and headed for the gate, which I had foolishly stepped in front of. There was no time to dash out of their path, but I turned sideways and the flock parted magically, like the Red Sea, although a couple of sheep mashed my toes in passing. The dog formerly known as Homer streaked past in a blur.

"We need to call him back," Carolyn called to me as he

whizzed along, his tongue nearly on the ground. "He's showing the long tongue. He's getting exhausted. Can you grab him?"

He'll come, I told her. "Homer, come to me, boy," I yelled. He stopped, looked beseechingly at me, took a step toward the sheep. "Come, now!" I said, more convincingly. He broke off the chase and came to my side.

"Good," Carolyn said, impressed again. "You don't know how important that is. One of the hardest things in herding with new dogs is the recall, to get them to stop herding and come. That's half the battle right there." I puffed up a bit. Of course my dogs would come to me. I wondered briefly if she was using positive reinforcement on me.

But, she cautioned, his "lie-down" was unacceptable. It was essential that the dog drop to the ground instantly, even when his herder was a long distance off. I had a lot of work to do.

Still, Homer was a natural. He'd passed his instinct test with flying colors. He was welcome any time, Carolyn announced, for whatever level of training and herding I wanted to pursue.

Then, of course, it was time for Devon, to whom nothing came simply. His fate was to always struggle for his place in the universe.

If Homer instinctively wanted to herd, Devon seemed excited but unmoored. When I yelled "Go get 'em!" he charged the sheep individually rather than herding them, going for chunks of wool over maneuvering or persuasion.

Where Homer encircled, Devon lunged. Where Homer barked and cajoled, Devon attacked. He was nervous, constantly looking to me for approval. Even I could see that he was off, out of sync. The contrast between the two performances was obvious; I felt for him.

Homer had the eye, Carolyn assessed, but Devon didn't yet. (This startled me—he sure had it for school buses.) That didn't mean he couldn't develop one, however. She watched him closely for another ten minutes, as he frantically raced from one end of the pasture to the other. He seemed rattled, as if he understood that this was something he ought to know how to do but couldn't master.

His look said: *Am I screwing it up? Is this right? Are you okay?* Every now and then, he'd leave the sheep and run over to rest his nose against my leg. He was still keeping watch, not over the flock but over me. He was also wheezing, nearly gasping for breath. I wasn't sure he liked this destiny stuff, now that he'd settled into a happy routine with me and Paula.

Still, it was exciting to see the dogs loping along, in their supposed element, as close as Jersey dogs would ever get to the moors and the flocks.

"Carolyn," I murmured as we left the pen, "can I say it? Just once?"

She looked briefly puzzled, then got it, laughed, and said sure.

I patted both dogs and gave them each a hug.

"That'll do, boys," I said.

❖❖❖❖❖❖❖❖

We closed up the pasture, got the sheep back into the barn, and Devon and Homer joined Dave in the shade, where there was a pile of hay and a bucket of water. Herding was more exhausting than I could imagine, Carolyn said, and dogs needed to rest after each round.

I could see that my two liked being with the guys, joining the lunch-pail crowd, taking a break, talking sheep. Dave was more welcoming now, wagging his tail in "attaboys." I reached into my pocket and, when I saw Carolyn busy with the sheep, slipped Dave another liver treat. He rolled blissfully over on his back again, eyeing my car.

Both my dogs had passed the herding instinct test, Carolyn told me. They could and should herd. She had to admit that she hadn't expected such strong instincts in Barbie collies. I could be proud of the recall. Their response to me was rare, she said, testament to the affection between us and the work we'd done together. I *was* proud of it, actually.

While Homer was a star, she continued, and could probably go into herding competition if I had any desire for that, Devon needed herding perhaps even more. This surprised me; I thought he might have flunked.

But Carolyn was reputedly one of those people who could tune in to a dog's spirit, read him through the work his instincts led him to. She worked to train aggressive dogs as well as herding breeds. She could quote studies on rats and wolves; she'd obviously spent years researching animal behavior.

"Homer is solid, grounded," she said. "But Devon can't quite make sense of the world."

He really only made sense of me. I was what he knew, what he trusted and relied upon, she explained; the rest of the universe remained a tangle, a jumble. Devon really didn't know how things operated, even his ancestral work, and was terrified of failing again.

Herding could possibly change that. It could settle him down, give him some peace of mind, Carolyn thought. She'd noticed signs of stress in him—his squinting and panting, his lowered ears—except when he was near me. Orders and commands unnerved him, triggering either anxiety or defiance.

Her reading of Devon was a perceptive one. But it saddened me, too. His trek wasn't over, it seemed; it might never be over.

So I signed the boys up for some classes. If I owed it to Devon to meet some sheep, I owed him even more the chance to make sense of the world. The herding world would be hearing, I warned Carolyn, from "Team Barbie."

❖❖❖❖❖❖❖❖

Life is deeply peculiar. The last place on the planet I would ever have expected to be, or that anyone who knew me would expect me to be, was in a pen, dodging enraged sheep and signaling frantically to two dogs.

But little more than a week after our audition, on another gloriously clear spring day, the three of us were back at Raspberry Ridge. Carolyn had set out two chairs and a bench alongside the sheep corral. Sensing perhaps that I didn't have Homer or Devon's quickness, she had worked up a show-and-tell for me.

Summoned by Dave, Carolyn came out of the barn carrying a worn tin box. My dogs had wandered up the hill, and she reached for the shepherd's whistle she wore around her neck and gave a short blast.

The sound was sharp but not piercing. Homer and Devon were at her side in an instant.

The three of us sat politely and attentively as she opened the tin container and pulled out four sections of two-inch-high plastic fencing, along with three small plastic sheep, a tiny herder, and two black dogs that closely resembled border collies.

Painstakingly, she closed the lid and began assembling the fence on the top of the container. Then she placed the plastic man—me, the herder—across from the two plastic dogs. In between she arranged several toy sheep, while discoursing on dog care and common training mistakes. (She didn't really agree with the throw-chain I carried and jangled to get the dogs' attention, for instance; a whistle was a lot more effective. The more she talked, the more I understood how little I really knew about dogs or their training. But, then, she hadn't lived with Devon for a year.)

This was her philosophy-of-herding lecture.

Homer and Devon sat on either side of me, transfixed, like teenaged hackers watching *Star Wars* for the first time, as Carolyn moved the little figures around to show the positions we would all shortly take.

We were going to work on balance, she lectured, the line between predatory instincts and working. Border collies are closely descended from wolves, and the sheep, dumb as they are, know they're not on the same team. It might get rough out there, she said, gesturing toward the paddock.

I was to enter a small pen that held about a dozen jumpy sheep while first one dog, then the other, raced around the perimeter. When the dog was across from me, with the flock between us, Carolyn would click a clicker and I would praise him extravagantly at that precise moment. The idea was to train the dog to position himself on the opposite side of the herd.

Carolyn demonstrated for me with her tiny characters. It was unnerving to grasp how much work was involved merely to maneuver the dogs into the right position, the one where they'd earn my praise. It wouldn't be easy, Carolyn cautioned, accurately. Devon and I exchanged glances, like warriors about to go into battle. Homer was already giving the sheep the eye, long-distance—a good sign.

I chained Devon a few yards away, then went into the pen, trying to look confident. Homer began tearing around in mad circles, never pausing for long, sometimes trying to jump the fence and sometimes trying to tunnel underneath it to reach the sheep. Once or twice he stopped across from me—the approved position—and Carolyn clicked and I shouted my appreciation. But he was obsessed with the sheep, paying only scant attention to me.

No problem, Carolyn said; he was quite young. He'd get it down. Once he figured out I was the gateway to sheep, he'd focus on me quite intensely. By the time Homer began to grasp the idea, however, he was spent—a virtually unprecedented condition. He staggered to the water bucket and collapsed. I chained him to the fence and released Devon.

I'd noticed, as Homer circled the pen, that Devon wore what I called his "raptor" look (as in *Jurassic Park*), silently scrutinizing Carolyn, me, Homer, and the sheep.

Of Devon's many odd traits, none impressed me more than his curiosity and determination to figure out how things work—how the refrigerator opens, what actions precede going outside for a walk, where I store the dog biscuits in the kitchen.

He'd been taking in this spectacle in almost every detail, and when it was his turn, he amazed both Carolyn and me. He circled widely around the pen—"squaring off"—coming opposite the herder, just as Carolyn had wanted.

Carolyn clicked, I clapped and cheered, and Devon did it again. I simply backed up behind the sheep, turned into position, gestured with one hand, and yelled "Go around!" and Dev rushed to the spot opposite me. Further vindication for the Barbie team. But after two or three rounds, Devon seemed to balk. Having shown that he could do it, he appeared less in the grip of herding fever, more afraid to mess up.

"Last week I wasn't sure, but he could be very good at this," Carolyn mused as we left the paddock. "I'm just not sure yet that he really *wants* to. But let's give him a chance. . . . It's striking how he concentrates and scopes all this out. He was really paying attention."

Homer, on the other hand, had no such ambivalence. Carolyn said he had a "spectacular" instinct for herding, one of the strongest she had seen in so young a dog.

Like the previous visit, it had been a strangely exhilarating afternoon for me, for the dogs, mostly for the three of us together.

The relationship had altered a bit already. Homer was less the deferential little waif; he was a working dog, his instincts rising in a powerful display. He had more respect for himself, and Devon treated him accordingly. For his part, Devon soon stopped trying to herd other dogs and lost much of his interest in trucks and cars. Once you've had a taste of the real thing, Carolyn explained, substitutes seem inadequate.

It inspires a bit of awe to see working dogs really do their jobs, to see thousands of years of history, instinct, and breeding well up and become manifest in a sunny pasture. It transforms the way an owner sees a dog, and the way the dog sees himself. This, perhaps, is the bond people talk about between working dogs and their masters. Working together in that paddock, I was aware of how much trust and communication it takes for a dog in full pursuit of prey to drop in a second at the wave of a human's hand, to move back and forth in response to his slightest body movement. And there were other, to me more meaningful, rewards.

I felt I'd kept my promise to Devon, that a debt had been paid and that the gesture was much appreciated.

❖ ❖❖❖❖❖❖❖

What might Old Hemp make of all this? Hemp, I'd read, had flashed like a meteor across the universe of sheepdogs. His confidence and demeanor were so pronounced, it was said, that sheep merely looked at him and instantly complied with his every request.

We were not in that league. Homer and Devon had ticked off

the sulky sheep, who remained fully aware, I'm sure, that it had really been Dave who'd moved them around, not me and my game amateurs.

I didn't know how long we would work at herding, or how successfully. This wasn't my destiny, and probably not Devon's or Homer's, either.

Old Hemp would have to forgive us if we loved hiking through county parks, visiting neighborhood dogs, dashing around upstate, chasing chipmunks, and plunging into crystalline ponds just as much.

⟡⟡⟡⟡ ⟡ ⟡⟡⟡⟡

The sun had begun to lower into the Pennsylvania hills as we drove away, planning to return. Carolyn, the faithful Dave at her side, waved her crook in farewell. I pulled over to a pasture fence and gave the gentlemen another good look at the sheep, who glanced back uneasily.

"Barbie collies, my ass," I said, scratching the dogs behind their ears. "Good guys. I'm proud of you."

They beamed back.

We are, I thought, two eminent dogs and one dangerous man.

POSTSCRIPT

Sometime after midnight, the full moon beamed into my cabin bedroom like a floodlight. I woke up, startled by the brightness.

Homer was sitting at the foot of the bed, staring through the window at the silhouettes of trees swaying in the wind. Shadows wavered across the blankets and the walls. Devon lay alongside me, instantly awake and alert, watching to see what was up.

I don't pass up a full moon on the mountain. It's a sight I never get used to or take for granted.

I got up, pulled a bathrobe over my flannel nightshirt, laced hiking boots onto my bare feet, and walked out onto the mountaintop. The cabin was chilly, but it would seem snug and warm after this encounter with the cutting wind.

The moon delivered as always, bathing the valley in cool light and casting shadows along the fringes of the meadow. The pastures and fields below looked like a muted quilt, with silos and farmhouses embroidered along the seams. If there were a full moon every night, I don't think I could ever leave.

The border collies, sensing a break in our routine, didn't dart out ahead of me as usual to scour the woodpile for chipmunks. They knew this wasn't our typical walk, maybe because of my odd outfit, perhaps because of the hour. They paced quietly beside me, waiting to see what the agenda was.

The moon was enormous, a giant silver plate right above us, thin clouds drifting across its face.

The wind came slicing up the meadow. I envied the dogs their imperviousness to weather. The winter, now finally giving way to spring, had been brutal.

The snow was gone now, but the trees were still bare. I clapped my hands and walked down into the meadow. It was too ungodly an hour to dress for a proper walk, but I wanted a brief look at this beauty to take back to bed, an aid to rest and lovely dreams.

This was the signal Devon and Homer had been anticipating; now they knew what to do. They loped down the open field, running easily on the stubbly grass to the stand of pines below, not chasing each other or anything else, just galloping along together in widening circles.

The dogs weren't working or hunting and they weren't playing; they were just traveling, free as the air in this open space.

Without quite intending to, I strolled over to Julius's mountain pew, the spot where he had always planted himself to regally study the panorama below. That afternoon, I had scattered his and most of Stanley's ashes on the mountain, some on that very spot. I'd saved some of Stanley's ashes to take to the Battenkill, where he'd learned to swim.

The truth is, I'd had enough mourning. I was weary of it. I'd answered too many questions about where the Labs were and what had happened to them; I'd explained their illnesses too many times and accepted too many condolences.

I'd wanted that afternoon of scattering the ashes to be dignified, low-key. I don't believe in an afterlife. I hope—and I've given my daughter and wife the appropriate instructions—to go the way Julius and Stanley did, without grueling operations and unnecessary machinery, a swift death followed by cremation.

But just in case I was wrong in my unsentimental view, I'd mixed some of Jules and Stanley's powdery ashes together, so that the two Labs could remain united.

Then I'd sat on the ground for a few seconds' silence. As usual, the border collies read my mood. Devon understands sadness intuitively; he rushed over and began licking my face. Homer, not normally interested in emotional dramas, rested his head against my leg. But there was little to say about Julius and Stanley that hadn't already been said and thought.

My dog year was winding down.

It was time to reclaim my more normal life, to focus more on my work, on people, and on other things I had, to varying degrees, neglected amidst the turmoil, training, grieving. "You should be proud of yourself," Deanne told me on the phone one night when I called with a Devon-and-Homer progress report. "What you did was hard to do."

It was, and I was, but it was still time to move ahead.

It had been almost twelve months since Devon had landed so explosively at Newark Airport, inaugurating this time largely defined by dogs, their arrivals and departures, their dramas and foibles, needs and wants.

If my dogs had been faithful to me, I'd been faithful to them. We'd all kept our promises to one another, and then some. I felt good about that.

People tell me all the time that they can't bear to get another dog because the pain of losing their previous one was so great. I know what they mean, but I don't share that feeling.

I wouldn't trade any of it, not for a second. When the terrible day comes that Devon and Homer have to go, in the rightful way that dogs live shorter lives and die before their human partners, my fervent wish is that my gimpy leg will carry me right back to Newark Airport to await the next crate.

It seemed from my moonlit perch that I had been ping-ponging through this canine universe for a long time, alternately stricken, anxious, patient, vigilant, angry. It felt almost ludicrous to have gotten so embroiled in the lives of four dogs.

Yet they had challenged me, invigorated and improved me; I had no doubt that I was better for it. For me, the challenge of middle age was not to stand still. Devon, in particular, made sure I wouldn't.

In a couple of weeks, I'd scatter the rest of Stanley's ashes on the banks of the Battenkill. Homer loved to splash and paddle there now.

Every now and then, tossing the old blue ball for Homer, I expected for a second to see Stanley charging madly after it. Or I looked for Jules in the corner of my study. But those moments were fewer now; in a while, they would stop altogether, as they should.

Watching these two new dogs circling in the meadow gave me a particular kind of happiness, though, rare and satisfying. The border collies looked so beautiful on that brilliant night: Devon sleekly jet-black and white, Homer having lost his puppy fluff and growing a glossy blue-tinged coat.

After a few minutes' meandering, I clapped my hands again. Devon, finishing his third or fourth arc across the meadow, froze and then turned, suddenly came back up the hill, Homer following more slowly and circuitously behind.

Devon was running strangely, for him, streaking in a straight path right toward me. I wondered for a moment if he'd glimpsed a deer or a fox behind me, he was traveling so purposefully.

He was almost upon me before I saw the look on his face in the bright night, saw that he was aiming straight at me.

I suddenly understood and threw my arms wide open. Dev leaped into the air and crashed into me, a forty-five-pound guided missile trusting, as my young daughter once had, that I would catch him. I staggered back against a wooden Adirondack chair that sits like a lonely sentinel on the crest of the mountain; it kept me from toppling over backward.

I could barely hold Devon's wriggling body as he lunged at my face, licking one cheek and then the other, his bright eyes fierce with love, small bits of leaves and burrs clinging to his fur.

My eyes were watering from the chill as we hugged, the wind whipping, Homer gamboling around us in circles, knowing something was up, but not sure what.

Once again there were three of us and we moved together like a school of fish. But this particular moment, this collision on the mountaintop in the dead of night, was for Devon and for me. The two of us had earned this hard-fought connection. We deserved it.

"We did it, boy," I said to the exultant creature in my arms. "We did it."

CAUTION

It's tough to meet—or read about—a border collie and not want one. They are beautiful, intelligent, storied dogs. Under certain conditions, you can have a wonderful relationship.

But acquiring a border collie can also be a major mistake, both for you and for a dog that looks great on cable shows but needs very particular circumstances in order to thrive.

Believe me when I say that this breed isn't for everybody. Border collies need hours of exercise; they can be unpredictable around small kids; they are hyper, obsessive, territorial, and weird. If you don't provide continuous and challenging work and exercise for them, they will find ways to busy themselves, ways you probably won't appreciate.

There are lots of working dogs and other breeds, including

happy and healthy shelter adoptees, that are much easier to raise and far better suited to urban and suburban life.

If you are pondering bringing a border collie or, for that matter, any other dog into your life, please consider it carefully and talk to breeders and other owners first.

AFTERWORD

On a hot, sticky day in June 2002, on the last day of a satisfying but grueling book tour, I pulled my truck over and let Devon and Homer out onto the western edge of the Mount Holyoke College campus in South Hadley, Massachusetts.

The school, emptied for the summer, was gorgeous, the picture of an atmospheric, tree-lined historic New England campus. It was also border collie heaven—vast, sloping lawns and paths populated by fat, lazy chipmunks and squirrels.

On tour, the boys and I had worked out a routine for controlled outbursts. They popped out of the backseat and went into the fabled border collie crouch, like wolves on the prowl, giving the creatures sauntering along the lush lawns the eye.

"Get ready," I said, and the dogs hunkered down, noses almost to the ground. Then I slapped my knee and yelled, "Go get 'em," and they took off, racing around trees and across lawns, circling back to me, always back to me. My role was to watch and smile, delighting in their energy and enthusiasm.

In fifteen minutes, their tongues were long enough to scrape the ground and they trundled over to gulp some water from a portable bowl I carried, then plopped down next to me on the grass for a breather.

It wouldn't be long before they were up again, though. This chase could continue for an hour, if I let it, squirrels racing up the trees for cover, chipmunks diving into holes or behind the shrubs. The dogs were fast enough to catch them, but they never did; the chase was the point of the game.

We had become amazingly skilled at finding small corners of the world where we invented neat stuff to do. The day before, stuck in a motel in the middle of vast urban highway sprawl, we'd raced from one traffic island to another behind a stretch of tacky fast-food restaurants. They couldn't have had more fun. Border collies are workaholics; their ability to find tasks in the oddest places still amazes me.

But today was different. "That's enough," I said, the signal to break off the chase. While I doubt that even my sophisticated dogs grasp concepts like book tours, I also know that they can read me. They stayed close by, licking my hand, resting their heads on my lap and my knee. Devon offered his paw; Homer rolled over for a belly scratch.

For the past three months, the book tour publicizing *A Dog Year* had taken us to a dozen different cities and towns. The tour had begun with a reading outdoors at a windswept sheep farm in Pennsylvania, followed three days later by a talk during a white-out snowstorm raging outside an old opera house in upstate New York.

We sat nose-to-nose with reticent farmers and working dog people at a cozy library in West Rupert, Vermont, and greeted dog owners at pet food fairs in New Jersey and Pennsylvania. There were bookstore readings and library signings in Boston, newspaper interviews and radio shows along the East Coast. We stayed at a variety of motels in different settings, from the oceanside to strip-mall wastelands. We even threaded our way through anti–World Trade Organization demonstrations in Washington, D.C.

The dogs and I had been together for every single event, from an after-dinner talk at the White Dog Café in Philadelphia to a sheep farm in rural New Hampshire under a reporter's watchful gaze, to encounters with hundreds of friendly strangers in bookstores. Everywhere, the dog people turned out to hear my story and share theirs.

It says something about how far I'd fallen into the dog world that weary as we all were, I was sad to see the trek end. We'd had a romp.

This was the end of it, the last day, the boundary between

A Dog Year and the coming year, between one book and the next. As I tossed the dogs bits of my tuna sandwich, I thanked them profusely and sincerely.

❖❖❖❖❖❖❖❖

Life with these dogs is never static. Since our first encounters with sheep in Pennsylvania, a lot had happened.

Carolyn Wilki and I had become good friends, and of course I'd grown addicted to sheepherding—a natural lure for brainy, odd obsessives like border collies and me. I spent hours out at her farm, drawn into the exhausting, smelly, relentless, and complex life of the shepherd. I learned to perform an array of new chores: pre-dawn grazing, midwifing during lambs' births, worming and shearing and tail-chopping, all the while continuing the painstaking process of learning to herd with my dogs.

Carolyn and I spent long evenings shooting the breeze about life, books, politics, and the world—and dogs, the conversations always seemed to come around to dogs, in front of her farmhouse, or out in the pasture.

Raspberry Ridge had become a wonderful vantage point from which to witness the drama of people and dogs. Apart from people wanting to learn herding, it also attracted a stream of troubled owners and their canine companions, some aggressive, others neurotic or traumatized. Watching Carolyn and other trainers cope with all their problems was an education. And I still needed one.

Devon and I were continuing the complicated process of understanding true patience, of curbing and channeling the anger and restlessness that resided in us both.

As I worked to become calmer, quieter, more accepting, Devon responded. I'm tempted to say he morphed into another dog altogether, but the truth is that Carolyn helped me bring out the good heart and sweet soul that were always there, waiting to emerge.

So much had changed—down to the name I called him. Carolyn had urged me repeatedly to change Devon's name. Given almost any command, she noticed, he cowered, winced, squinted, or turned away, all signs of stress and avoidance, echoes from his unhappy past.

Having learned to trust her instincts about such things, I overcame my resistance and rechristened him Orson, after one of my cultural heroes, Orson Welles. The name "Devon" had always been a bit Martha Stewarty for my tastes anyway.

I thought the transition would be difficult but with the help of some liver treats, it turned out to be a snap. I simply made eye contact, repeated his name—"Orson"—and popped a liver treat into his mouth. After only a couple of bags, he'd swivel his head at the sound of the word. And the impact was striking: He actually came when I said, "Orson, come," and lay down when requested. His ears stayed up, and the squinting and cowering stopped. As he became more responsive, I grew more relaxed myself, more trusting.

He could still push my buttons now and then, but the shouting and chasing receded from our relationship. He no longer saw much point, I guess, in dashing down driveways, pursuing school buses, or roaring off without permission after squirrels, field mice, or neighbors' cats. And I wasn't reinforcing this mischief by constantly yelling at him and calling attention to it. We had actually learned how to communicate.

Homer, always the anti-Devon, was Lab-like in his sweetness and easygoing nature, his deference to his older pal, and his affection toward all beings except sheep. Unlike the Labs, however, he proved to be a working dog through and through. He lived to herd, and taught me to love herding with him. He was the monarch of the pasture.

Each morning, he stared at my closet to see whether I was putting on my ordinary shoes or, if he were lucky, my herding boots. One night, while staying at Raspberry Ridge—we were often there for camps, visits, seminars, lessons, and practice sessions—I awoke to find the door to my room ajar. Orson was sleeping next to me on the bed, but Homer was gone. I ran out with a flashlight and found him lying next to the sheep pen, keeping an eye on his flock. He could never be around sheep enough.

In a way, it was fortunate that Orson had not yet taken to

herding—though he did love to run ineffectual circles around the occasional sheep or goat—because it gave Homer and me something that was ours, that forged a quiet, non-spectacular but very powerful partnership. Every now and then, Orson's powerful and ingrained instincts broke out, and he began herding with me, or breaking out into one of those spectacular border collie outruns around the sheep that are so breathtakingly beautiful. Carolyn said she was certain these instincts would continue to emerge. She insisted that I not give up. In July 2002, I took him into a field with a dozen sheep, and he swept out around them, breaking into a businesslike, professional trot, wearing back and forth much like the working dogs I'd seen at trial, driving them right up to my feet. I knew Carolyn was right, and I'd wait until he was ready.

Homer had won several trial ribbons, but our best times came out in the pasture with Carolyn's flock, watching the sun rise or fall, staring up at meteor showers, all of us listening to the sweet crunch, crunch, crunch of the grazing herd. Orson had learned—slowly and reluctantly—to accept that his role here was subordinate, to be still, at least for the moment. But he loved coming along even when that mean playing unaccustomed second fiddle to Homer the Herder.

Besides, Orson had his own contributions to make. The Parks Department supervisor in my town had called me up earlier in the spring to ask if the border collie he'd heard about might be of some help in clearing a gaggle of willful geese out of a local park where kids played soccer and baseball. Sure, I said. I had just the dog.

We spent many happy mornings there persuading the geese to take their yucky droppings elsewhere. Orson was born for this work (so unlike sheepherding that it sometimes confounded Homer). On command, he'd tear after the nearest group of geese, circle and bark until they took off, then head for the next circle. He never tired, never felt intimidated by their hissing and flapping and pecking, never gave up. And he didn't have to master the complex rituals of herding; his love of the chase, limitless energy, and persistence did the job. Over a couple of weeks the goose population fell from eighty to just ten holdouts, a number the town could live with.

Orson was happy to take on other creatures, too. Upstate, I'd gotten a call from a local farmer who'd heard that I had "workin' " dogs. Could we possibly help round up some semi-domesticated cattle beyond his farthest pastures, who'd holed up in their private corner of the woods for several years? Sure, I said. I had the perfect dog.

A few miles up the county road, we saw our quarry. Orson bounded out of the truck and into the woods, heading straight for the biggest cow at top speed. Almost instantly, the dozen renegades were stampeding toward the safety of their barn, Orson staying adroitly out of kicking range while, um, encouraging them to move smartly along. The farmer, who'd rolled up on his tractor, looked impressed and handed me a $10 bill; he had work for us anytime we were around, he said.

We didn't have be around livestock to have work, though. We invented elaborate games with frisbees and balls. We were just as happy and busy in an abandoned Massachusetts industrial park as we were in the country. Every walk was busy and purposeful. In between the two of them patrolled my yard for passing dogs, rabbits, and sanitation department trucks, racing back and forth along the fence until a brick-hard dirt path edged the lawn. Only at night did some mysterious and invisible switch click off, and the dogs collapse in various corners of the house. Orson slept in our bedroom, Homer in the hallway where he could gaze out the back window, ever in search of sheep.

I had learned so much. I saw everything about dogs and their relationships to people differently now.

Meanwhile, in the most basic way, Orson and Homer kept challenging me to get off my butt, to keep learning, changing, moving. And I kept trying to rise to the call.

Looking at my watch, I saw it was time to head to the Odyssey Bookshop in South Hadley, the last stop on our tour. "Let's go to work, gentlemen," I announced, and the two went bounding back toward the truck. They had this bookstore drill down pat.

"Which one is Devon?" was invariably the first question

people asked, but they usually figured it out even before I could respond. He was the leader, the captain, the greeter, the one who muscled smaller Homer aside to stick his nose in outstretched hands, to put his head in inviting laps, to claim two of the dog biscuits people brought along before Homer could get one.

Devon/Orson was an attention addict by now, a polished performer, intent on soaking up all the affection in a room. Homer waited patiently for his older brother to settle, then made the rounds for pats and treats of his own.

They greeted every fan, a number of whom had e-mailed me about the book and their dogs, then circled behind the podium, curled up, and fell asleep. They understood the protocol: say hello, scarf up the goodies and the pats and the coos, then doze while I droned on. We'd done this from Washington, D.C., to Philadelphia to Boston to New Hampshire. When the talk was ended, and the applause began, Orson sprang to his feet, barking, taking his bow. At the signing table, they mingled politely until every book buyer had gotten a signature (I was learning to enscribe copies not only for the reader but for King, Lucky, Bitsy, or Cocoa as well) and shown me photos of his or her dogs and left. *A Dog Year* was my eleventh book, but I'd never had such warm book signings, more like family gatherings than literary events. "I would've brought a picture of my dog," one shy woman told me in Petersborough, New Hampshire, "but I didn't know it would be so friendly-like." The Odyssey signing was just as friendly-like, a fitting conclusion in a famous bookstore to this odd journey.

Because it was so beautiful and we had such a long drive back home, I stopped back at the campus for a final workout. The boys disappeared behind a vine-shrouded lecture hall; I could hear small creatures shrieking. But Orson and Homer didn't run for long this time; perhaps, like me, they wanted to get going. It was time.

So into the car and home. I couldn't wait to see what they had in mind for me next.

ACKNOWLEDGMENTS

I thank my wife, Paula Span, who has shared this dog year and who spent so many hours reading and editing the first few versions of this work. As a friend pointed out, I am lucky in marriage and in dogs.

I am grateful to Deanne Veselka, owner and breeder of Wildblue Border Collies in Lubbock, Texas, for sending Devon and then Homer to me, and helping me to learn how to live with them. She opened a new world to me. I will take great care of her dogs.

I thank Dr. Brenda King for helping me face reality and deal with it compassionately; Ralph Fabbo for teaching me how to train dogs; and Carolyn Wilki for propelling me to the next level.

I am grateful to Kathy Hansen, Jon Stemmle, Karen Stohl, and the staff and students of the University of Minnesota School of Journalism and Mass Communications, who welcomed Devon and me for a month and made us feel they were just dying for an odd border collie to hang around.

I deeply appreciate my neighbors and friends in Montclair, New Jersey, who make owning a dog a communal pleasure. I appreciate, too, my non-dog-owning neighbors' forbearance at the not uncommon sight of manic border collies tearing across their lawns after a cheeky squirrel.

Ruth Coughlin has provided great support, friendship, and encouragement. So has Jeff Bates.

Brian McLendon has been a valued friend who provided encouragement and feedback. And thanks to Margaret Waterson, a friend and the co-owner of Battenkill Books in Cambridge, New York, who listened patiently to my stories about Devon and the Labs and suggested I ought to write them down. Bruce Tracy is much appreciated for his patience and deft editing.

I am very grateful to Richard Abate of ICM for taking me and this book on.

And I owe much to my daughter, Emma Span, for existing, for puncturing my balloons, for sharing my bizarre humor and my love of terrible movies and of the New York Yankees. She reminds me every day to keep laughing at myself and at life.

Jon Katz
Jackson Township, New York
June 2001